ADVA
RELIGIOUS AND BUSINESS LEADERS FOR

God Wants You to be Wealthy

"If you want to know about real wealth, read this book."

> **Mark Victor Hansen,** Co-author of the best selling:
> *Chicken Soup for the Soul* series and *The One Minute
> Millionaire: The Enlightened Way to Wealth*

- "The greatest strength of the book is the content, particularly
  P.I.E.S. and the scriptural evidence, both of which are very profound and useful.
- The other strength is the motivational language, which suits the
  book, is your natural style, and is truly convincing.
- I think even a secular audience, and certainly a wider Christian or
  even "religious" audience would enjoy the book. Your interpretation of the Scripture examples is actually very appealing even to
  secular folks.
- Lastly, and unfortunately, I did not put my 'kudos' in the text wherever I like what you did. But you should know that many times I
  wanted to put a big checkmark and say, "excellent point!"

> **Launie Gratto,** Editor and Book Critique,
> Effectivewriter.com

"This book teaches principles and ideas that will change your life. A
must read for those who want God's wealth, God's way."

> **Robert G. Allen,** Millionaire Maker and Trainer, Best
> Selling Author: *Creating Wealth, No Money Down,
> Multiple Streams of Income,* and *The One Minute
> Millionaire: The Enlightened Way to Wealth*

- "Good book—well researched and interestingly written.
- Good title—catchy and relevant to the needs of many people,
  especially African Americans and other "minorities."
- High degree of enthusiasm—seems like the coming together of
  many years of thought and presentations.

- Scholarly—credit is given to your research sources.
- Written with authority—you are in full command of your subject.
- Shows a high degree of concern for your readers and persons who can profit from your message.
- Doc, you have written a good book. It has come from your head and heart. . . . go on and publish it. Your work will enhance the lives of many people."

> **Dr. Bennie Goodwin**, African American Theological Scholar, Educator, Author, Editor, and College and Seminary Professor

"There is a way to obtain good success and that way is in Christ. A true believer understands that when we are blessed, it only promotes and confirms the Word of God. Dr. Hammonds, in his unique and intellectual way, navigates the reader through this book and challenges us to a higher dimension of spiritual and financial expectancy. Only if you are prepared to escape the "community called average" should you read this book. This book has been designed for the forward thinking individual who has foundational security in God and believes that; 'If God can do anything, He will do everything. There simply is nothing too hard for our God.' "

> **Valerie Daniels-Carter**, CEO and founder of the country's largest African-American–owned restaurant franchise [V & J Foods Holding Companies Inc.], which controls 96 Pizza Huts and 41 Burger Kings throughout the midwest and New York. It is a company with 3,500 employees and $92 million in annual revenues.

For more advance acclaim from readers and editors, see the last pages of the book.

GOD WANTS YOU TO BE:

"Wealthy in every way, so that you can be generous in every way, producing with us great praise to God."

The Apostle Paul
2 Corinthians 9:11
(*The Message* translation)

To Charlene,
a woman of God
& the word.
May God's Wealth
Be Yours in
Every way!

God Wants You to be Wealthy

How to Release the Wealth Builder Within

 *A Wealth Commentary*

KENNETH HAMMONDS, M.DIV., ED.D.
THE SUCCESS COACH

SEP

Spiritual Empowerment, Plus
Publishing Company

Published by Spiritual Empowerment, Plus Coaching Company, Inglewood, CA.

Scripture quotations marked "NKJV" are taken from the New King James Version. Copyright © 1982 by Thomas Nelson, Inc. Used by permission. All rights reserved.

Scripture quotations marked (NIV) are taken from the *Holy Bible, New International Version*®. NIV®. Copyright ©1973, 1978, 1984 by International Bible Society. Used by permission of Zondervan. All rights reserved.

Scriptures quotations marked (NLT) used in this publication are taken from *The Holy Bible New Living Translation*. Copyright 1996, Tyndale Charitable Trust.

Scriptures quotations marked (NRSV) used in this publication are from the *New Revised Standard Version Bible*. Copyright 1989 by the division of Christian Education of the National Council of Churches of Christ in the USA. Used by permission.

Scriptures quotations marked (The Message) are from *The Message: The Bible in Contemporary Language*. Copyright 2002–2003 by Eugene Peterson, NavPress a division of The Navigators, U.S.A. Used by permission. All rights reserved.

ISBN: 0-9716989-2-9

Manufactured in the United States of America.

DISCLAIMER
The information in this book is for educational purposes and spiritual growth purposes only. The publication is distributed with the understanding that the author/publisher is not engaged in rendering legal, accounting, medical, or any specific financial advice. The author accepts no liability for the actions and consequences that the reader may incur and a result of taking actions as a result of this information.

Contents

God Wants You to be Wealthy

A Message to My Readers

Thank you for your desire to read, interact, grow, and expand through this unique book: *God Wants You to be Wealthy*: *How to Release the Wealth Builder Within*. *God Wants You to be Wealthy* is a scriptural, motivational, and spiritual perspective of wealth and how to build wealth in your life. It is also: a wealth commentary of the Bible, a declaration of spiritual and economic empowerment, and a book about honorable wealth building.

You will appreciate the exploration on one of its underlying themes: the compatibility of spirituality and wealth, or more specifically, the spirituality of building, enjoying, and sharing wealth. In Part One: Spirituality and Wealth, we will explore the natural harmony of spirituality and wealth, then for the rest of the book, show you how to create and enjoy this symphony.

A Wealth Commentary of the Bible

God Wants You to be Wealthy is the **first wealth commentary**. First, because it's the first work (to my knowledge) to apply a systematic wealth approach to the Bible. A *wealth commentary* comments upon and interprets Scripture and life from a *wealth perspective*. This viewpoint recognizes the universe and humankind as creatures of a God of great abundance and wealth in His nature and works. This wealth viewpoint also considers the various facets of human society as God's vehicles for assisting humans in being wealthy and successful spiritually, emotionally, intellectually, relationally, physically, materially, financially, and occupationally, and in every aspect of human endeavor. Indeed, this commentary sees wealth everywhere—in the Bible, in the universe, and in you.

This commentary on wealth is the result of a thirty-year personal journey into the development of a Christian success and wealth mindset.

My personal journey began with a praise of lack and poverty but ends with the joy of discovering God's plan for humans here on Earth—that they create and enjoy wealth. For me, the Message of *God Wants You to be Wealthy* is not merely an academic exercise or the hollow chatter of another motivational book: it is a Calling, a Divine Imperative, I must fulfill.

A Declaration of Spiritual and Economic Empowerment

God Wants You to be Wealthy is not just a book—it's a declaration of spiritual and economic empowerment, a personal declaration of independence to ignite the release of the underutilized and undervalued wealth builder within. Wealth builders are those who can imagine, identify, manifest, and persist in the production of wealth for every dimension of life. Wealth builders embrace the spiritual value *and* the earthly utility of wealth. We all have a powerful wealth builder within, and together we will explore how to uncover it, release it, and direct it toward the development of full wealth in your life.

I am presenting this message of empowerment to all. God wants all to be wealthy, regardless of the circumstances of their lives. Yes, ALL: grade school children and teenagers wanting to supplement their allowance; young adults taking their first steps into the world of money; middle-age adults in transition; the success-minded senior adults and the physically, emotionally, or mentally challenged who struggle to believe God is not through with them yet; every race and ethnic group, every man and woman, and every nation on Earth. There are, however, requirements for producing and enjoying this wealth, and that's what this book is all about.

Honorable Wealth Building

The Scriptures teach that God wants you to be wealthy. But, let me emphatically state: Yes, God *does* want you to be wealthy, and God wants you to *build* wealth. But, God wants you to build wealth and be wealthy the right way, the honorable way—His way. This is not about wealth stealing or wealth exploitation. It's about the personal development of one's own God-given gifts, knowledge, and experiences to discover, shape, enjoy, and share God's wealth.

The bold message I present is *not* about greed, selfishness, or riotous living. It is *not* about narcissism or any other *ism.* (narcissism [NAR-se-siz-em]: Being extremely self-centered and wrapped up in oneself.) *God Wants You to be Wealthy* is about wealthy thinking and living out God's original plan and purpose for you and for all the people of this planet.

Your Unique Personal Touch (UPT) in Building Wealth

The second underlying theme of the message "God Wants You to be Wealthy" is that not only does God want you to be wealthy, but also that God has given to each of us the power of a Unique Personal Touch (UPT) in building wealth. Each individual conceived and born into this world is extraordinary and has a Unique Personal Touch.

Your UPT is the special style, way, design, or system of behavior that you've been given to touch the lives of others and to display God's beauty to the world. With your UPT, you show the world who you really are in your work, art, speaking, and living. Your UPT is the result of a complex mixture of your experiences, knowledge, natural gifts, and skills, which brings that special "you" to all you say and do.

God has given you permission to use your UPT in creating wealth; indeed, it is the only way you can create wealth. As we shall discuss later in Chapters 1 and 2, humankind was uniquely designed for this purpose. Oh, the joy of being YOU!

However, some of you may not, at this point in your life, enjoy being you. But, it is my hope that through the pages of this book and through the touch of the Spirit, you will applaud yourself and enjoy developing and presenting your UPT to the world.

Our UPT is the way we add quality and wealth to our lives and to the lives of those we touch. How your experiences, knowledge, gifts, and skills directly impact your ability to produce wealth is more fully developed in Part Two: Releasing the Wealth Builder Within.

Who this Book is For

Everyone does not receive my bold declaration, "God Wants You to be Wealthy." I've noticed when I say this declaration to "ordinary" people—especially some Christians—they immediately get defensive and ask questions like, "What do you mean by wealthy?" or "Well, I'm not so sure about that." This is no book for *ordinary thinkers*.

One well-meaning Christian man upon first hearing this phrase immediately rejected it, not even attempting to hear me out. He then went on an impassioned outburst about the errors and foolishness of wealth. He went so far as to send me a book and audiotape about the errors in the book *The Prayer of Jabez*, by Bruce Wilkerson. Thus, I have come to the conclusion that this book is *not* for everyone.

On the other hand, whenever I mention the phrase to entrepreneurially minded and business people (Wealthy Thinkers), they all respond exactly the same: "Oh, I know that!" Or, for others contemplating this powerful truth for the first time, the light of revelation comes upon them and they say, "Yes, I receive that!"

This message seems to especially speak to success-minded individuals and budding entrepreneurs—those who wish to launch new businesses and create new wealth. A primary focus of my ministry/business as a success coach is to support beginning entrepreneurs and *solopreneurs* (solo business owners and home-based business owners). I assist them in building business skills and making the life adjustments necessary for success.

Beginning female entrepreneurs will find portions of this work especially designed for them. I present the woman in the Bible (2 Kings Chapter 4) in two chapters and apply the principles of entrepreneurship to the life and business of this poor single mother with two children.

In its widest scope, this book is for all those with a desire to be more productive financially and who have an urge to create greater success in their lives. It will help them properly link spirituality and wealth building and assist them in developing the thinking, skills, and success strategies needed to experience positive change, clearer direction, and abundant growth in their lives.

So, wealthy thinker, keep on being productive and fully embrace the message, "God Wants You to be Wealthy." By the way, don't miss receiving the Wealth Benediction at the end of Part Four—it's for YOU!

God's Wealth Cycle: P.I.E.S.

God Wants You to be Wealthy presents an empowering wealth-building perspective called, "God's Wealth Cycle: P.I.E.S." (P.I.E.S. stands for: *Producing* Wealth, *Increasing* Wealth, *Enjoying* Wealth, and *Sharing* Wealth.) This new wealth cycle perspective provides the foundational system to free people, communities, and nations from poverty thinking and behavior to powerful actions for creating and enjoying wealth and a life of abundance. Details of the wealth cycle are presented in Chapter 5.

The Format of This Book

KH Quotable Quotes
I have included personal quotations at the beginning of each chapter and occasionally also within a chapter. Each reflects on wealth and success thinking. I call these quotations KH Quotable Quotes. They range from the obvious to the somewhat profound. I hope you will enjoy them and can utilize them in your daily living. Sometimes, I use a quotation from another author. I call this simply, A Quotable Quote.

A Word about Bible Translations
Throughout this scriptural study of wealth, I use various translations. The fresh interpretations and insights of different translations help bring the ancient biblical text alive for the modern day reader.

Having been trained in theology, philosophy, and biblical Hebrew and Greek, and in ministry for over thirty-five years, I am fully aware of the need to be faithful to the text and to the God of the Bible. I joyfully embrace the evangelical tradition of honoring the Word of God and the God of the Word. I have referenced over 200 carefully chosen and thoroughly researched verses of Scripture and nearly all are fully quoted. I am proud of the biblical basis and thoroughly biblical nature of this commentary.

I also offer insights from the original biblical languages with my own translation or paraphrase based on the original Hebrew or Greek text. Frequently, in the discussion of biblical texts, I'll use the term *literally,* or the terms *Greek* or *Hebrew.* These terms refer to the actual or additional meanings of the original language.

Listed below are the abbreviations for the various Bible translations used in this work:

KJV: King James Version
NIV: New International Version
NKJV: New King James Version
NLT: New Living Translation
NRSV: New Revised Standard Version
OT, NT: Old Testament, New Testament

Logo

In the chapter and section headings for the rest of the book, I will use the logo below to signify the book title, *God Wants You to be Wealthy.*

May you enjoy wealthy reading, thinking, and living.

Go to my Web site, WealthyThinking.com, and sign up for my free email newsletter entitled, *Wealthy Thinking.* It is a monthly motivational wealth newsletter for wealthy thinkers ONLY!

PART ONE

Spirituality and Wealth

 A KH Quotable Quote ∞

Wherever there is active spirituality,
there is wealth.

The challenge is to activate spirituality so that
the true wealth of God can be revealed.

∞∞∞

Command those who are rich in this present world [wealthy
people of faith] not to be arrogant nor to put their hope in
wealth. . . . Command them to do good, to be rich in good
deeds, and to be generous and willing to share.

1 Timothy 6:17, 18 (NIV)

CHAPTER 1

Spirituality and Wealth?

In this chapter, we will discuss:

✦ Harmony or Conflict?
✦ Faith and Wealth: A Biblical Example
✦ God: The Source of Wealth
✦ The Universe: God's Masterpiece of Wealth
✦ Wealth: Our Inheritance

Harmony or Conflict?

To be spiritual is to use wealth and justice to build a better world;
to be demonic is to use wealth and injustice to destroy it.

Spirituality and wealth—in harmony? Unlikely. Unthinkable. No, impossible! These are the thoughts of many regarding these seemingly opposing superpowers. For many, if you are spiritual, you hereby renounce all worldly possessions and take the spiritual "vow of poverty," heading off to serve the Lord with no distractions from the nasty material things of this world. "It is better to serve God than money," so they say, quoting Jesus' statement in the Gospels. "Blessed are the poor," they again quote Jesus. They miss the point. Jesus is cautioning us about *serving* wealth, not *having* wealth. And as far as blessing the poor: when you're poor, you need a blessing *and* some money!

So with this as their starting point, many people curse money and wealth and embrace a poverty mentality. Well, I'm here to set the record straight about wealth and spirituality. When wealth is properly understood and utilized, it becomes a powerful force for good—God's source for good. Every ministry and human endeavor has a need for wealth and money. The word *wealthy* will be clearly defined and thoroughly dealt with in the following chapter. For now, let's define *wealthy* as simply *having more than enough (abundance) of something valuable.*

However, many make the mistake in not understanding wealth as more than money and not understanding the need to possess wealth in every area of their lives. In Chapter 2, I will discuss 10 dimensions of wealth that can be attained in the human experience. All these areas are important, but the emphasis of this work is upon the development of your gifts, talents, and skills to produce the financial health and wealth that are natural for humankind. It's using the wealth *within* you to manifest the wealth *around* you. Wealth is everywhere. It may not be discerned by the naked eye, but for spiritual eyes the presence of wealth is clearly visible, permeating every corner of this planet and every atom of the universe.

Faith and Wealth: A Biblical Example
Abraham, the Father of Faith, Wealth, and Tithing

Spirituality and wealth—are they really compatible? The answer is a resounding, YES! The faith and wealth discussion starts with Abraham. The Scriptures declare Abraham as the great father of faith in the living God and the father of those who believe. (Romans 4:11–12, 16–18; Galatians 3:7) Today, we are yet enjoying this great spiritual heritage. This heritage was passed on to us from Abraham's descendents who wrote the Bible, the great prophets, and finally through his greatest Son, Jesus Christ, the Messiah.

Abraham is the Father of Wealth. He's the first person in the Bible to be called *rich* or *wealthy*—probably not the first to possess riches, but the first significant person in which there was the spiritual harmony of faith **and** wealth. In Chapter 5, we will establish Abraham as also the Father of Tithing (Giving wealth to God). Thus, Abraham is at once the Father of Faith, Wealth, and Tithing. He is the model for wealthy people of faith today. As a matter of fact, Abraham is described as *very wealthy*.

Abram was very rich (NIV: very wealthy) in livestock, in silver, and in gold.
Genesis 13:2 (NKJV)

The scriptural account of the spiritual resolve of this man of faith and wealth is awe inspiring. Spiritual and wealthy; is that possible? Yes! In Deuteronomy 8:18, God promises believers the ability to produce wealth to fulfill the covenant He swore to their fathers. Our spiritual father, Abraham, was materially wealthy and he was the father of the spiritual seed to follow. Yes, spirituality and wealth *can* go together. No, rather, spirituality and wealth are **obligated** to join forces.

God has placed within many believers the desire to produce wealth for themselves and share it with their families and the world. That honorable wealth desire within is NOT just some selfish idea outside the Will of God.

It is admirable to aspire to utilize your talents and abilities to create wealth for the world. As a matter of fact, it's better for the virtuous to be rich than for the world to be in the hands of those who don't support the causes of justice and righteousness. Better a man of faith and strong moral fiber to be rich than a man of cynicism, skepticism, and feeble ethical principles.

In the next few sections, let's establish God, the universe, and humanity as wealthy. For if the Spirit of the Universe is wealthy and the universe and Earth are wealthy, then there is no incompatibility of wealth and spirituality, only a discord regarding how this awesome spiritual force is used or abused by humankind. Properly linking wealth and spirituality brings to the human experience a beautiful harmony, not a cacophony.

God: The Source of Wealth

The subject of wealth starts with God, not man. God is the source of wealth, and God is wealthy in His nature, attributes, and works. God places invisible wealth in human beings, which empowers them to produce visible wealth in the world.

Oh, the depth of the riches [Greek = wealth] both of the wisdom and knowledge of God! How unsearchable are His judgments and His ways past finding out!

Romans 11:33 (NKJV)

And my God shall supply all your need according to His riches [Greek = wealth] in glory by Christ Jesus.

Philippians 4:19 (NKJV)

The translated word *riches* in the above passages is the Greek word *ploutos* which means wealth, riches. Since the words in both the passages above are singular, I prefer the translation wealth rather than the plural riches. As a matter of fact, the Interlinear Greek New Testament of the NRSV prefers my translation. It translates Philippians 4:19 as, "according to His wealth in glory."

Furthermore, the Romans 11:33 passage is a beautiful and vivid description of God's nature when literally translated, *Oh, the inexhaustibility of the wealth of God!* The apostle Paul here is overwhelmed when he thinks on the infinite nature of the Almighty God of the Bible.

Consider another attempt of Paul to describe the wealth of God in Ephesians 2:7: *That in the ages to come he [God] might show the exceeding riches of his grace in his kindness toward us through Christ Jesus.*

The magnitude of God's wealth is variously translated in the different Bible translations of this verse.

> KJV, NKJV: the exceeding riches
> NRSV: the immeasurable riches
> NIV: the incomparable riches
> The Bible in Basic English: the full wealth
> NLT: the incredible wealth
> Wesley's New Testament: the transcendent riches

So, God's wealth, according to these Bible translations, is exceeding, immeasurable, incomparable, full, incredible, and transcendent. Human words fail to adequately describe the vast wealth of the nature of God.

God is not a god of poverty. NO! God is the God of abundance and wealth. God's nature and attributes overflow in richness, wealth, abundance, and diversity. Since God is abundant, it stands to reason that His creation—the universe and the planet we have been planted on—would likewise be rich in resources. This vast universe receives its wealth from God.

The Universe: God's Masterpiece of Wealth

The heavens declare the glory of God; and the firmament showeth his **handiwork**.

Psalm 19:1 (KJV)

*By His Spirit He **adorned** the heavens;*

Job 26:13 (NKJV)

*His Spirit made the heavens **beautiful**.*

Job 26:13 (NLT)

In the beginning, God created the universe. God's universe is wealthy in every way: its age, size, and number of galaxies and stars (billions multiplied by billions). Scientists now count the stars of God's universe with a new number series called googolplex. It is the number 1 followed by 1,000 zeros! The universe's fantastic physical processes, mathematical precision, and its harmonious blending of cycles, colors, and rhythms leave us in awe as to its superabundant nature. God is AWESOME and everything He does happens in a BIG way.

God then began to work specifically on planet Earth to prepare it for the crowning creation of the universe—humanity. No other planet is naturally suitable for humanity's home. Our Earth is abundant in every detail necessary for the human life cycle, the environmental cycle, and the cycle of wealth.

The Earth is wealthy in its animal, plant, and mineral resources. The life forms that have been and are a part of this planet possess a rich diversity. Human classification systems have cataloged 1.4 million species of plants, microorganisms, mammals, and fish. However, this 1.4 million is only about 10 percent of the entire planet's species.

In 1998, the value of just the copper, lead, and zinc production in the USA alone was 4.5 trillion dollars. John Avanzini, in his book *The Wealth of the World*, estimates the 8 major minerals alone will produce 51.4 trillion dollars of **new wealth** in the world economy.

Gold and silver are not in the Earth by accident or chance. Their presence is designed by God, and they are here to help fulfill His purpose for humankind. The gold, silver, minerals, and animals belong to God. We don't own anything. We are caretakers, stewards of this great mineral and animal wealth. God has graciously allowed us to enjoy the abundant variety of creation and has commissioned us to utilize it for human good, enjoyment, and progress.

The silver is mine, and the gold is mine, saith the LORD of hosts.
Haggai 2:8 (KJV)

We humans are born into a wealthy universe and placed on a planet of rich resources. We must have been designed for wealth.

Therefore, since you were designed to experience life in an affluent environment, you were born to be wealthy. Indeed, every human being was born for this purpose. Yes, there are enemies that will challenge your prosperity. However, this opposition does not change the fact that God's *original intent* for his human creation was to: enjoy a wealthy relationship with Him; enjoy wealthy relationships with one another; enjoy the wealthy resources of this planet; and enjoy the fruit of our labor and our purpose. This is God's Original Wealth Plan.

The misuse of wealth by some does not invalidate the divine nature of God's Wealth Plan any more than does the abuse of the Name of Jesus invalidate the reality and divine nature of the work and person of Jesus Christ. Nor does abuse of power by the clergy of the Church invalidate the necessity and divine nature of the work of the Church. Human error in behavior does not negate the purposes of God; it merely vividly portrays the need for the plan of God to be fully realized in the human heart and human society.

Wealth is the *natural human condition.* Poverty, or lack, is an abnormality, a deviation from God's wealth standard. Just as physical health is also the natural human condition, but sickness, deformities, and abnormalities are deviations from God's health standard.

When poverty moves in, the Will of God moves out. Financial poverty is an economic deviant. Spiritual poverty and sin are religious deviants. Broken relationships are relational deviants. Greed is a material deviant. All these are deviants from God's Original Plan.

Wealth: Our Inheritance

This picture is part of Michelangelo's ceiling painting, *The Sistine Chapel,* in the Vatican in Rome, Italy. This is from the painting depicting the creation of Adam. The hand of God is on the right and the hand of Adam on the left. (Painted sometime between 1508 and 1512.)

To be fully human is to be wealthy and successful, continually reaching for the highest potential within. We have inherited wealth and success from our fathers: God, our Heavenly Father and Creator; Adam, our earthly father who was the first human to bear the image of God; and Abraham, our spiritual father of faith and wealth. Wealth is undeniably a human inheritance.

As inheritors, we have many valuable possessions passed on to us. We are inheritors of the wealth and abundance in our universe and Earth. We are also inheritors of the vast wealth of resources *within* all human beings: the magnificent image of God, the limitless human imagination, and the human brain—that great mental genius within.

The Image of God

This reflection of God brings to humanity a wealth of inner strengths and godlike qualities, including: mental abilities, spiritual sensitivity, emotional sensitivity, creativity, innovation, potentiality, and self-discovery.

The Limitless Human Imagination

This powerful human quality brings to the human experience the ability to form a mental picture of a future not yet present and a possibility not yet realized. With it, humans can imagine a new invention, create a wealth-producing product, or visualize enjoying a prosperous life in a safe, clean, and wholesome environment.

The Human Brain

This is the *most* fantastic creation in the entire universe and it brings brilliance and diversity to the human experience. The cerebral cortex of the human brain (only we humans have it) is the great mental genius within and what it is to be fully human. The cerebral cortex gives us *language*, *logic*, and *love*. From it also issues other higher cognitive processes and artistic expression.

You possess a wealth of mental genius inside of you. Educational studies confirm that human beings are born intelligent. However, as the infant grows, the negative forces of environmental factors and human systems begin to impact the child and she or he begins to deteriorate in natural intelligence. Don't pray for more intelligence—just use the intelligence you've already got! This inheritance of the image of God, the limitless human imagination, and the human brain is a winning partnership. So that makes you a winner!

∽ A Quotable Quote ∾

The human brain is the most complex creation in the universe
—and you own one!

—**Bob Grinold**

Wealth is the natural state of our universe, God's nature, and human existence. Spirituality and wealth *must* coexist. A spirituality without financial power is a weak piety that has never learned how to (or has been denied access to) tap into the full wealth of God's nature and human nature. And wealth without Spirit is wealth without a soul.

Yes, the beauty and symmetry of this universe demand human admiration. The universe is God's *handiwork* (Psalm 19:1). The Hebrew word implies that it is His poem; the universe is God's poetry in action. But, you know what? You, too, are God's poem in action. For Ephesians 2:10 (KJV) declares, "For we are his workmanship (*poiēma* in Greek), created in Christ Jesus unto good works, which God hath before ordained that we should walk in them."

The NLT says, "We are his masterpiece." You are the *magnum opus* of God's wealthy nature. Magnum opus means the greatest work of art. It is used to designate an artist's greatest legacy. A magnum opus demonstrates the creator's finest and most brilliant thoughts and craftsmanship. You are God's magnum opus. What is your magnum opus to humanity? Is it yet to be revealed?

"You are Simply Marvelous!"

I will praise You, for I am fearfully and wonderfully made; Marvelous are Your works, And that my soul knows very well.

Psalm 139:14 (NKJV)

Through the psalmist, God describes His intricately complex, gifted, and brilliant artistic creation called "human" as *marvelous*. Yes, you, the masterpiece of God, are Simply Marvelous! I know some of you thought a famous actor said this phrase first, but God said it long ago and you can believe it today.

You are a God-given original—genuinely unique and wonderfully made. The writer of the Psalm above, King David of Israel, was an avid naturalist and observer of human nature and the human condition. He uses the word *fearfully* to describe the formation of the living human body and human being. The Hebrew word for fearfully in this verse means *reverently*. The word *reverent* implies a respectfulness and tenderness of feeling which gives a sense of awe. It also implies some intrinsic value in the thing revered. God has created you with reverence and a sense of wonder. You are awesome: uniquely, reverently, and wonderfully designed.

You are simply MARVELOUS! You can say, "God made me and then broke the mold!" You are wealthy far beyond your present level of comprehension and you are simply marvelous! Say to yourself out loud right now, "I'm simply MARVELOUS!" As a matter of fact, if you need a positive message for today, go look in the mirror right now and say to yourself, "I'm simply marvelous!" And you know what—**you really are!**

"I'm
Simply
Marvelous!"

So, there is no divorce between spirituality and wealth. Indeed, I wish to unite them in holy matrimony and spiritual bliss for eternity. For Spirit and Wealth are eternal—they are the essence of God.

"SPIRITUAL" MISSION WORK AND WEALTH

Almost all the missionary activity (spiritual work) of the Church, especially work in third world countries and for those in poverty in this country, comes from a *wealth perspective.* Yes, we do take the Gospel of Jesus Christ with the spiritual promise of eternal life to foreign lands, but we also take medical doctors, nurses, educators, engineers, carpenters, and other specialists. Bringing these skilled professionals and eager volunteers along on the mission trips is our attempt at improving the quality of life for the people we serve.

We believe God wants them to do better and be in better condition than before we arrived. We are, in essence, saying that God wants them to experience a greater measure of spiritual and material wealth, health, and happiness.

Essentially, we present to them the message, "God Wants You to be Wealthy." Everything we do should be from a wealth perspective. We are to have the same heart for people that Mordecai, one of the great ancient leaders of Israel, had when he saw the plight of the people. Esther 10:3 (KJV) says Mordecai was *seeking the wealth* (the Hebrew word, *tov,* means good) of *his people.* Like Mordecai, the spiritual missionary efforts of the Church also seek the wealth of the people.

CHAPTER 2

Understanding True Wealth

In this chapter we will discuss:

✦ True Wealth
✦ The Bible: A Wealth Commentary
✦ Defining Wealth
✦ The Purpose of Wealth

True Wealth

*To be poor is unnatural; to be wealthy is natural;
to be spiritual is to be supernatural.*

*G*od wants your life to be full and overflowing with true wealth, blessings, abundance, and richness. Wealth in only the material realm is *not* the true fullness of wealth. Material wealth *by itself* is a sad thing. It is limited and will only take you so far, and usually not far enough. For, to be materially wealthy but relationally poor is to miss the real joy of life—loving and being loved. To be materially wealthy but mentally and emotionally bankrupt is to miss the joy of happiness and peace of mind.

On the other hand, if you declare yourself to be spiritually rich, but are so deeply in debt that you spend your waking hours avoiding bill collectors and other people to whom you owe money, then you are missing the joy of God's financial blessing. To declare yourself "spiritually rich" and have no inheritance or substance to leave to your children or to righteous causes is also to miss out on God's plan for human existence.

So, what exactly is *true wealth*? True wealth is *godly wealth*. Godly wealth is God-given, God-driven, and God-honoring. True wealth acknowledges that God's original wealth plan includes both the spiritual and material realms. True wealth also includes enjoying a plentiful quantity AND quality of life, liberty, and love. Plentiful means, *plenty-full*. That is to say, more than full—the supply is so full it is running over.

The Scriptures Regarding Godly Wealth

God-given Wealth
Moreover, when God gives any man wealth and possessions, and enables

*him to enjoy them, to accept his lot and be happy in his work—this is a gift
of God.*

Ecclesiastes 5:19 (NIV)

*Bestowing wealth on those who love me [God's wisdom] and making their
treasuries full.*

Proverbs 8:21 (NIV)

God-Driven Wealth
God-driven means God-inspired and God-empowered.

*But remember the LORD your God, for it is he who gives you the ability to
produce wealth, and so confirms his covenant, which he swore to your forefathers, as it is today.*

Deuteronomy 8:18 (NIV)

God-Honoring Wealth
*Honor the LORD with your wealth, with the firstfruits of all your crops;
then your barns will be filled to overflowing, and your vats will brim over
with new wine.*

Proverbs 3:9,10 (NIV)

Godly Wealth Brings Joy to the World, Not Sorrow
*The blessing of the LORD brings wealth, and he adds no trouble to it.
[NKJV: . . . and He adds no sorrow with it.]*

Proverbs 10:22 (NIV)

God Wants You to be Wealthy

We might also ask, "What does the phrase, *to be wealthy*, mean?" To be
wealthy means to enjoy a prosperous life of spiritual and material well-
being. Therefore, the phrase, "God wants you to be wealthy" simply
means that God wants you *to enjoy a prosperous life of spiritual and material well-being.*

The box below illustrates "to be wealthy" and includes both the spiritual and the material areas of life.

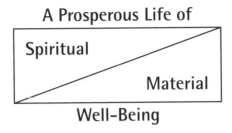

The Bible: A Wealth Commentary

Although not commonly recognized as such, the Bible is a book of wealth. God's Word is also a word to humanity about how to live and prosper. It is the best wisdom ever penned by man. The Bible is, indeed, a wealth and success manual. It is a wealth book. It's been a bestseller for hundreds of years and millions have used it to prosper their lives, families, countries, and their business and financial well-being.

It is ancient in its manuscripts of the past, but ever-modern in that its principles of wealth building and preservation still ring true today. In that sense, it is as current as the financial pages of the *Wall Street Journal,* the *Investor's Business Daily,* or *Barron's.*

- ✦ It is an impressive book, full of literary wealth.
- ✦ It is an influential book, describing spiritual wealth and inner wholeness.
- ✦ It is an indispensable book on the subject of building wealth and enjoying the life God has given to each human being.

The Word of God is applicable for successful living in every area of life. The Bible is a wealth commentary because it comments on, interprets, and explains the true nature of a life of wealth. (See Appendix One, *The Bible as the Wealth Book*).

The Scriptures have much to say about wealth. In the next section, we will present wealth commentaries of two Christian apostles, John and Paul, as they speak on prosperity and wealthy living. Both of these commentaries will further advance our understanding of wealth in a comprehensive and dynamic way.

Defining Wealth

Webster's Basic Definition

Webster's Seventh Collegiate Dictionary defines wealth as, "An abundance of valuable material possessions or resources, an abundant supply."

An Expanded View of Wealth: Its English Root Word, *Weal*

The word *wealth* is from the English word *weal,* which is derived from the Old English word *wel.* Weal (root word for wealthy) refers to a sound, healthy, prosperous state—one's well-being, or simply, to be well. This expanded view of wealth starts with the basic view of wealth as having more than you need (of something valuable), and then it also expands to include *plenteousness.* Plenteousness suggests that which is fruitful, productive, and abundant. So, in this expanded view, wealthy living would therefore mean a life that is fruitful, productive, and abundant. Just as the primary meaning of heal-th means to be healed or in a state of physical prosperity, weal-th (wellth) means to be well or in a state of financial and life prosperity.

Godly Wealth: A Holistic View of Wealth

Finally, godly wealth in the biblical view is comprehensive and holistic, for it not only includes the concepts of valuable material resources, a prosperous well-being, a plenteous life, and financial prosperity, but also advances the concept of wealth to include spiritual wealth. Spiritual wealth means a sound, healthy, and prosperous inner soul and spirit— one that includes rich fellowship with the living God and generous service to others. All of this is true wealth, *godly wealth.*

John's Prosperity Prayer

Beloved, I pray that you may prosper in all things and be in health, just as your soul prospers.

3 John 1:2 (NKJV)

Let's look at each important word or phrase in this little prayer, giving special attention to the meanings of the original Greek NT wording.

Beloved

Beloved is the Greek word *agapēte*, whose root word is *agapē* (ah-GAH-pay)—love. This word addresses Gaius as one who is *worthy of love, beloved* (one who was and is now continuously loved). It is a term of deep affection and can even be translated by the affectionate word, *dear*. The NIV and NLT translations of this word best give us the portrayal of it. They translate this word as, *dear friend*. Thus, the apostle writes a letter to Gaius and utters a prayer for his dear friend.

I Pray

The Greek word here means to pray or to offer prayer. But, it also means to wish, desire, or want. The KJV translates it as *wish;* other translations prefer, *pray*. The NLT says, *I am praying*. The basic idea of this word is to express a wish or desire in the form of a prayer. In this prayer, John expresses a wonderful desire for the recipient, Gaius.

That You May Prosper

The Greek word here for prosper is composed of two words: *good* (prosperous) and *journey* (trip). It is similar to our saying to someone traveling, "Have a nice trip!" Only it is stronger in that it literally means to have a prosperous journey. It refers to being successful and prosperous. Biblical resources further advance its meaning as, *to be furthered or prosperous temporarily or spirituality*. God wants you to have a prosperous journey in life. Don't you want that, too?

In All Things

I'd like to draw special attention to the NKJV translation, *in all things*. This translation captures the essence of the underlying Greek text. The idea is not *above all things* as the KJV indicates, but rather concerning all things or simply, in all things. That is to say, I desire that you prosper in all

Resources: *The New Analytical Greek Lexicon*, by Perschbacher and *The Spirit-Filled Believer's Topical Bible Reference Edition*, from Harrison House, researched by Dick Mills.

things means in every area of life, in **every dimension** of human existence.

God wants us to prosper in every area of our lives, not just the spiritual. God does not want any area of your life untouched by prosperity and wholesome living. Isn't that empowering? God's love and care extend to every road in the journey of our lives.

Some commentators draw attention to the three-fold prosperity mentioned in this verse.

+ Prosper in all things (material wealth)
+ Be in health (physical wealth)
+ As your soul prospers (spiritual wealth)

From this viewpoint, the verse declares prosperity spiritually, physically, and materially. The three-fold prosperity view is illustrated below. Spiritual wealth is the center of human life.

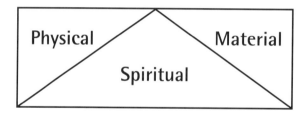

So, God is saying to us today through the apostle John:

"*I want you to enjoy a prosperous life of spiritual, material, and physical well-being.*"

Or, more simply: "*I want you to be prosperous in every area of life.*"

Paul's Prosperity Prophecy

And God is able to provide you with every blessing in abundance, so that by always having enough of everything, you may share abundantly in every good work.

You will be enriched [Greek = wealthy] in every way for your great generosity, which will produce thanksgiving to God through us.

2 Corinthians 9:8, 11(NRSV)

In verse 8, the apostle declares (prophesies, predicts, pronounces) a blessing upon the poorer Christians in Corinth who have given so generously to the relief effort for the Jerusalem saints. Because of their unselfish giving, Paul assures them of God's ability to provide an abundance of every blessing so they will have enough of everything. Because, if they don't have enough, they, of course, cannot *share abundantly in every good work.*

In verse 11, Paul also pronounces wealth upon the members of this congregation. The English verb *enriched* is a combination of two French words, *en* meaning in, inside, within, and *riche* meaning rich or wealthy. It literally means then: *to impart wealth within.*

The Greek word in verse 11 translated, *will be enriched* in the NRSV, literally means "to make wealthy." This word and the following phrase can be translated, *being made wealthy in everyway*; again, **every dimension of life**.

The Message translation of 2 Corinthians 9:11 poetically declares that God wants you to be:

Wealthy in every way,
so that you can be generous in every way,
producing with us great praise to God.

Being wealthy to be generous: what a spiritual concept! The emphasis here is not upon spiritual wealth only. Indeed, spiritual wealth is the *foundation* of the wealth the believer receives. However, it is also the *channel* through which wealth, abundance, and success will flow into every dimension of life.

Of course, this word from God is valid for us today. Through these Scriptures addressed to first-century individuals, God is saying to all humanity, "I want you to be wealthy in every dimension of life."

Both Scriptures above, 3 John verse 2 and 2 Corinthians 9:8, 11, emphasize true wealth, which seeks success and prosperity in each of the ten dimensions of human life. The box on the next page illustrates this.

WEALTHY IN EVERY WAY
Wealth in All Ten Dimensions of Human Life

SPIRITUAL (Godliness)	INTELLECTUAL (Mind)	EMOTIONAL (Moods)
MATERIAL (Things)	FINANCIAL (Money)	PHYSICAL (Healthy Body)
SOCIAL (Relationships)	OCCUPATIONAL (Work, Productive Activity, and Your Vocational Calling)	TIME (Time Management, Goal Setting, Dreams)
ENVIRONMENTAL (The complex combination of social [*the type of people around you*], cultural, climatic, and living surroundings)		

Since the Ten Dimensions are central to an understanding of the true wealth God wishes for us to enjoy, it is important to more clearly define each dimension of wealth. As you read each definition ask yourself the question, "How can I enjoy a greater depth of wealth in this dimension of my life?"

Spiritual Wealth is a sound, healthy, and prosperous inner soul and spirit—one that includes rich fellowship with the living God and generous service to others.

Intellectual Wealth is being rich in life-long learning and discovery. It's the joy of discovery and the quest for knowledge and wisdom.

Emotional Wealth is being rich in sanity: happiness and peacefulness of mind. It's inner contentment even when things seem to not be going according to your plan.

Material Wealth is having the things you need to make your life safe and comfortable. It's the physical expression of the wealth of your mind.

Financial Wealth is having more than enough money for your financial independence or financial freedom. It's enjoying financial stability in abundance.

Physical Wealth is health (strength, vigor, and wholeness) in your physical body. It's usually the result of deliberate care and maintenance.

Social Wealth is the real joy of life: fostering and enjoying positive, wholesome relationships with people, the community, the nation, and the world. It's loving and being loved.

Occupational Wealth is doing what you love and having the joy of being able to express your special Calling and gifts. It's the full expression of your UPT (Unique Personal Touch, see, Message to My Readers) to the world. It can be the enjoyment of either voluntary or employment based productive activity.

Time Wealth is enjoying the trek toward the fulfillment of your dreams by daily goal directed action. It's success: enjoying the journey, not just struggling for the destination.

Environmental Wealth is having wholesome, peaceful living surroundings that stimulate personal growth and a healthy lifestyle for your physical and emotional well-being. Indeed, it is promoting a healthy surrounding that will foster growth and safety in every dimension of your life.

The environmental dimension of life is often overlooked. But it is extremely important, and foundational to all the other dimensions. Environment is that powerful influence upon an individual that greatly determines her or his survival and significantly shapes or *misshapes* the level of affluence.

Sometimes when I'm coaching individuals, I'll have them observe, clean up, and organize their living surroundings. Occasionally, changing just this one factor in their lives gives them more energy and tranquility of mind. P.S.—Have you checked your environment lately?

True wealth means abundant living in every dimension of human life. God has created us for this purpose.

Wealthy Materially and Financially

What does it mean to be wealthy materially and financially? Why would a Christian even desire to be wealthy in these areas? You may say, "I just want enough to get by." First, let me state the foundation of what it means to be materially and financially wealthy. The initial foundation of wealth materially and financially is ownership. Ownership *brings* freedom.

Wealthy individuals are owners with freedom and money—this gives them their power. However, the money is only a by-product of their ownership. Many have said, "Money is power." However, money's power is only temporary if it does not include ownership. That's why when people get money they then seek to own something—land, buildings, houses, transportation, or other possessions. Every expression of riches in nearly every culture is founded upon ownership.

So, the wealthy person's foundation consists of:

Ownership ⟶ Freedom ⟶ Money = Power

So, why all this discussion about ownership? Well, I want you to understand that it is not money just for the sake of money that should be important to you. Life is not about money. Seek and work for ownership. Ownership is not only the first step in material wealth—it *is* material wealth. With ownership comes control. That's why renters will always be at the mercy of and the control of owners. Want freedom? Get ownership. I'm sure you know that the word, *landlord* means, *master* of the land. Therefore, if the landlord is the **master**, what does that make you as the *renter*?

It is all right and preferable to have things. Just don't let things have you. Why wouldn't God want people to have ownership of possessions—houses, clothing, transportation, etc.? Even Jesus Christ's family owned a home and had transportation. His robe was so valuable that at his crucifixion the soldiers had a little Las Vegas style gambling sweepstake to see who would win the prize. It's nice to possess nice things.

Everything in God's temple in the Old and New Testaments was the best—gold, silver, and the finest wood and tapestry—because wealthy also means possessing that which is of good or excellent quality.

I don't believe God wants us to have rags for clothing and junk for houses. I believe God wants us to have ownership of the things in this world. Oh yes, we may need to start off renting, but our aim should be possessing, owning. This is the beginning of wealth. That is the only way we can be free to live and free to be. You know the Scripture that says, *The rich rules over the poor, and the borrower is the slave of the lender, Proverbs 22:7 (NRSV)*

So, slave or ruler—which are you? Better yet, which do you desire to be? Our greatest example of faith, Abraham, was an owner. Indeed, God approves of faithful, responsible ownership.

Financial wealth means having money enough for your financial independence or financial freedom. Millionaires define financial independence as, *where your passive income exceeds your desired lifestyle needs.* That's wealth. One of the ways you can tell if you are financially wealthy is: if you never received another regular paycheck, would you be financially able to meet all your financial obligations and still have funds left over?

Passive income, of course, means receiving money from your ownership and/or past work that still bring in revenues from your investments, business income, product sales, etc. So, being wealthy financially is the result of many years of work and intelligent money handling. It is the fruit of your labor.

Wealth is financial attractiveness. One of the laws of financial attraction is: *people who produce, invest, and own are attractive financially.* You become wealthy by becoming a producer-investor-owner rather than merely a consumer-spender-renter.

In order for the believer to give, she or he must first possess and own. You can't place a homeless individual or family in a house you don't own or don't have the money to pay rent for them. You can't supply Bibles to people in foreign countries unless you can purchase them. If you only have just enough to get by, you'll never have enough to help anyone else. In order to assist others with their needs, you will need wealth—*more than enough.*

The Purpose of Wealth

Since God has placed within human beings the desire and ability to produce wealth, what is its purpose? Simply put, the purpose of wealth is two-fold: for God and for good. That is to say, wealth's purpose is to glorify God and to do good for (to help) mankind.

The Two-fold Purpose of Wealth

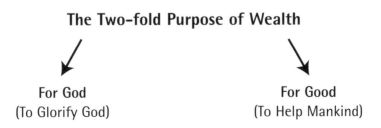

For God
(To Glorify God)

For Good
(To Help Mankind)

Wealth's purpose in helping mankind can be further broken down into four areas:

+ To assist in meeting human needs
+ To move human cultures and human life forward to a better future
+ To help alleviate human suffering and pain
+ To spread justice (righteousness) throughout the world

Wealth is good and important because it is:

+ From God.
+ God's blessing to the world.
+ God's way of showing love to His creation.
+ God's plan for dealing with the many ailments of humanity.

A KH Quotable Quote

Wealth is not a luxury; it's a necessity.

Thank God for this teaching about wealth in the Scriptures, about well-being and soundness of spiritual and material resources. For no resources are more valuable than those from God—whether spiritual or material. Biblical teaching concerning wealth balances the poverty mind-set and the greed mindset with a biblical view of true wealth.

I trust you will rid yourself of the poverty mentality that believes God wants you to be poor. That's simply NOT true! God wants you to have a prosperous well-being. He wants you to have a healthy state. Yes, God wants you to enjoy wealth in every area of your life—true wealth. Many people who espouse the teaching that poverty is for you are themselves doing well. They believe God has called some to poverty, sickness, and pain, but not them!

We have seen in this chapter the scriptural foundation for the title of this wealth book. It is founded upon the wealth prayer in the letter written by the apostle John to his dear friend Gaius and in the apostle Paul's prosperity prophecy to the Corinthians. So, in case you had been wondering, "Is it scriptural? Is it true?", now you know for sure. *God Wants You to be Wealthy*. He said so Himself!

PART TWO

Releasing the Wealth Builder Within

  A KH Quotable Quote

Think you're poor;
think you're wealthy.
Either way—you're right.

But be ye transformed . . . by changing the way you think.

Romans 12:2 (KJV, NLT)

CHAPTER 3

Ten Wealth Building Secrets of a Millionaire Mom

In this chapter we will discuss:

✦ A Single Mother Who Discovers Ten Wealth Building Secrets

Errata: Pages 42, 44, 46, 49, 54
(NKJV) should be *(NIV)*

A Mother with Two Kids, No Job, No Husband, and No Special Skills Finds the Wealth Builder Within

When you've got ideas and enthusiasm,
you've got the keys to wealth.

But, when you've got action and persistence,
you'll open the door.

There is an exciting story in the Bible (2 Kings 4:1–7) about a widowed single woman who came to the prophet Elisha after her husband died. She came pleading for a handout but left with much more. Read the story below from the NIV.

The Story

The wife of a man from the company of the prophets cried out to Elisha, "Your servant my husband is dead, and you know that he revered the LORD. But now his creditor is coming to take my two boys as his slaves."

Elisha replied to her, "How can I help you? Tell me, what do you have in your house?"

"Your servant has nothing there at all," she said, "except a little oil." Elisha said, "Go around and ask all your neighbors for empty jars. Don't ask for just a few. Then go inside and shut the door behind you and your sons. Pour oil into all the jars, and as each is filled, put it to one side."

She left him and afterward shut the door behind her and her sons. They brought the jars to her and she kept pouring. When all the jars were full, she said to her son, "Bring me another one." But he replied, "There is not a jar left." Then the oil stopped flowing.

She went and told the man of God, and he said, "Go, sell the oil and pay your debts. You and your sons can live on what is left."

We first meet this woman in an impoverished, destitute state. Unfortunately, her situation is an all-too common experience of millions of women in the USA. The plight of women and men in the world's poorer countries is even more devastating than the American experience. So, many people with seemingly no special talents, abilities, or education are left to figure out how to make ends meet. They also spend much of their efforts keeping their children from being enslaved by crime, poverty, and early fatherhood or motherhood. It becomes a major life challenge just keeping their young daughters and boys from becoming school dropouts or drug addicts.

What's a *non-gifted* person to do? The prophet, Elisha, gave the answer in this story, and it still remains valid in these modern times. The main idea of the story is how this seemingly *untalented* woman of extremely limited resources found courage and resourcefulness within. With encouragement from the prophet/coach, she reached deep within, acted upon her "little" inner resources, and produced enough wealth to get herself out of massive debt.

We'll meet this woman again in the next chapter, when we look at how beginners can produce wealth. From her situation, we glean many powerful principles necessary for financial and entrepreneurial success. She learned how to release her wealth builder and discovered a fortune!

In this chapter, you will learn the principles that motivated this single, uneducated woman to become a creator of wealth rather than a victim of poverty. Like the woman in this story, you have suffered long enough with lack of abundance. It's now time to enjoy the blessings of God's wealth. It's your season. You are an inheritor of wealth.

The Wealth Continuum

Before we move to our story, I'd like to introduce my model of economic levels called the *Wealth Continuum*. The Wealth Continuum is a series of six abundance/financial levels from poverty to wealth. Below is a visual representation of the Wealth Continuum concept. Where are *you* among the six levels in the movement from poverty to wealth? As you move up, so will those you touch along this path to wealth. The six levels are:

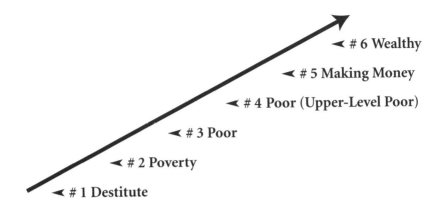

For more details and descriptions of each level of the continuum, see *Appendix Four.*

This uneducated single mother of two was stuck in level one (destitute, extreme poverty, and overwhelming debt), but when she enthusiastically utilized the wealthy resources within her, she was able to move to level six (wealthy).

A central purpose of *God Wants You to be Wealthy* is to help you tap into your inner resources to build wealth as did the woman of 2 Kings 4. It will also inspire you to experience the highest level of wealth you desire, as you move upward through the abundance/financial levels toward wealth.

In our story, Elisha the prophet understood the power of the wealth builder within and started this woman on her journey up the Wealth Continuum by showing her how to produce wealth, enjoy it, and share it with her family. These powerful principles are also available for you today.

Let's follow this woman along her journey to the top of the Wealth Continuum in a verse-by-verse motivational commentary. The prophet Elisha's advice to her is a wonderful example of the power of looking deep within oneself to release the wealth builder and produce wealth. This story is the most outstanding example of wealth creation in the Bible and this woman is the greatest wealth builder in the Bible. She went from less than nothing to great wealth.

Below is this story in terms of ten wealth building secrets. The word, *secrets,* means these are principles, actions, or ideas not often utilized effectively. They are also governing directives that work in any culture, community, or at any stage of life. These secrets are at the center of this fantastic story of success and wealth creation. They will work for married people, single people, young, and old. They'll work for you. You can apply them in your life today, as you seek to get out of debt or produce wealth for some other reason: to buy a car, a house, or anything else you desire.

Ten Wealth Building Secrets: The Most Outstanding Example of Wealth Creation in the Bible

The Single Mother of 2 Kings Chapter 4:1–7

Wealth Building Secret # 1:
Get out of debt; stay out of debt.

Verse 1 (NKJV)
The wife of a man from the company of the prophets cried out to Elisha, "Your servant my husband is dead, and you know that he revered the LORD. But now his creditor is coming to take my two boys as his slaves."

The man of God was in debt and then died. (Did he die from the weight of his debt?) The problem was, he left no inheritance or provision for his wife and two sons. I see here a man who is very spiritual but also negligent in his duties as a father and provider for his family's welfare. He left no inheritance for his family; what an insult to his wife and sons!

However, worse than that, he left them with an overwhelming amount of debt. The debt was so great that the creditors were going to seize his sons and make them slaves. Are you so spiritually minded that you are of little earthly good? If you are a spiritually minded individual, you will use all of God's resources to take care of your earthly obligations.

I also see a man who was unwise in his use of money. He was in extreme debt, and being in debt is not good. And if you are in debt, first do everything possible to avoid further debt. Then, use your God-given wealth creation ideas to reduce and eliminate your debt.

It was the burden of heavy debt that drove this widow to become a beggar. Heavy debt and little or no income will pressure you to do things that were previously beneath your dignity. Have you ever been so low on funds that you were forced to do things you normally just wouldn't do? Such is the life of one in debt. (Yes, I've been on that road.)

I have noticed that God cannot fully use someone in ministry or in life when he or she is deeply in debt. Remember, debt is bondage. Individuals in debt are limited in what they can do because the burden of debt is always hanging over them. But, when one is debt free, the mind is also free. When you are debt free, you are also free from the strong temptations of the Devil luring you to steal to pay off your debt. You are also freer to give to the people and organizations you believe in. However, when you are barely making ends meet, life is difficult and the temptations are stronger.

The practice of slavery or imprisonment for unpaid debts was a legal and accepted practice during Old Testament and New Testament times and also accepted in our more modern times. People in England were placed in debtor's prison for unpaid debts into the late 1800s.

We are not told the amount of the debt owed on the two boys, but an example in a New Testament story told by Jesus has a man placed in prison for owing 100 denarii (about $8,400, representing 100 days of labor). If this woman owed something like this for her two boys, she may have owed $16,000 or more to her creditors, which represented nearly a year's wages. But, whatever the amount, it was overwhelming for her financial condition. It might as well have been a million dollars, for she was destitute and unable to care for herself and her boys. She certainly could not pay any amount of money to relieve this debt.

A modern parallel to the ancient story is the modern story in the fantastic bestselling book, *One Minute Millionaire*, by Mark Victor Hansen and Robert Allen. This inspirational and practical book is two books in one volume. On the right-facing pages of the book is the story of a single mother with two children whose children were taken away from her. She must raise $1,000,000 in cash within 90 days to keep them. How she struggles and strategizes to reach this goal is a fascinating story. On the left-facing pages of the book is the discussion of practical principles and strategies needed for creating wealth and financial freedom.

Wealth Building Secret # 2:
Use what you have, no matter how small it may seem.

Verse 2 (NKJV)
Elisha replied to her, "How can I help you? Tell me, what do you have in your house?" "Your servant has nothing there at all," she said, "except a little oil."

This mother and wife who was now thrust into an unexpected life of single parenting and extreme poverty was asked by the prophet, "*What do you have in your house?*" She at first replied, "*Nothing, there at all.*" But, then she thought about it and said, "*Nothing, except a little oil.*" I'm sure she also thought, "Why is this man asking me this? Why doesn't he give me some money or just take up a collection from the associates of my husband? Why doesn't he just take some money from the treasury? My husband gave many years and much money to this ministry. Come on, Elisha; give me some money. That's why I'm here. I'm not here for silly questions. My husband is DOA (Dead On Abundance—no abundance and no inheritance), and I need some money!"

This was the perfect time for God to act through this woman. God had something better than a mere handout for her. It's better than a good welfare system. For either of these would have limited her income and never given her a chance to learn of her own God-given abilities.

When asked by the prophet about her resources, this single mother replied she had, "*nothing except a little. . . .*" Maybe you feel as though you, too, have "*nothing, except a little. . . .*" You may have so little you feel you have nothing. However, all you need is a little. All miracles start with one of two ingredients—a little or nothing. So, if you've got only a little or nothing to work with, then you're at the first step to a miracle.

Remember the story of the little boy with only two small fish and five small loaves of bread in John Chapter 6? Nothing there, but a little here—a little boy, a little lunch, and a little money. One of the disciples, Phillip, said a year's salary (modern day equivalent of about $20,000) would not be enough to buy food for the large crowd. Wow, talk about needing a miracle!

However, Jesus is naturally cool in this crisis situation. John 6:11

(NLT) says, Jesus "gave thanks to God" for this little lunch and it turned into a banquet feast for over 5,000 people! No telling what God will do when you give Him thanks for even the smallest blessings in your life.

Don't look for a mere handout, but the empowerment to utilize your gifts. Empowerment is part of Phase Four of the P.I.E.S. cycle— Sharing Wealth (caring for and empowering others). Remember, P.I.E.S. stands for Producing Wealth, Increasing Wealth, Enjoying Wealth, and Sharing Wealth. This is God's Wealth Cycle (More details about P.I.E.S. in Chapter 5).

Are you a single mother? Are you a young adult seeking a new career that will utilize your talents? Are you unsure of what your talents are? Are you a mature and experienced adult who is employed at a job that is not fully utilizing your EKG'S (Experience, Knowledge, Gifts, and Skills)? Has someone told you that you can't do it? Has someone predicted you'll always be at the bottom? Well, if you're able to read this book, you're also able to release *your* wealth builder and live a life of financial success.

Are you a senior adult or in some way handicapped or unable to do what you want to do? Do you believe that you have nothing to offer the world and that your best days are behind you? Wake up to your God-given greatness! You may not be able to do the things you used to do, but then again, you don't have to! You can get others to do the things you don't want to do or can't do. You don't have to be young or perfect; you just have to be committed to letting God use you.

The jar of oil represents the resources and talents this single mother possessed which she had never before considered. In the next chapter, we will go into more detail concerning how to produce wealth by utilizing the talents within.

What resources do you have that you've not considered using? You may say you have too little talent, ability, or skill to be a powerful wealth builder. But a little is all you need. What little (scarce) commodity do you have in your life that you can give to God? Do you think He will multiply it? Is there wealth "in your house"? Have you overlooked what's inside you? Don't exclude even the smallest things you have around you and in you. God can use anything.

Wealth Building Secret # 3:
Go into action; obey God.

Verse 3 (NKJV)
Elisha said, "Go around and ask all your neighbors for empty jars. Don't ask for just a few.

This woman will now learn to work with what she already knows. The prophet said, "Go, get into action; obey God." She knows about oil and she has a network of contacts (neighbors).

So, the prophet in just one little statement has shown this single mother the resources she has never acknowledged (knowledge about cooking oil, a network, and a potential market). This woman has wealth "in her house."

Wealth Building Secret # 4:
Pray, plan, and prepare in private.

Three principles for producing wealth (4, 5, and 6) occur in verses four and five :
"Then go inside and shut the door behind you and your sons. Pour oil into all the jars, and as each is filled, put it to one side."

She left him and afterward shut the door behind her and her sons. They brought the jars to her and she kept pouring.

Verses four and five have a call and response, or a call and echo effect. Verse four states the prophet's advice and verse five echoes her positive responses. She did exactly as the prophet instructed and for this she was rewarded with abundance.

Prophetic Advice and Coaching:
Then go inside and shut the door behind you.

The Woman's Response and Follow Through:
She left him and afterward shut the door behind her.

The prophet asked her to get alone with herself and her family where she could pray, plan, and prepare for abundance privately. You can't tell everyone your great ideas for abundance and blessing. Many just won't understand. Are you preparing for abundance or looking for failure?

This woman's little family business starts off with private discussion and prayer. The power of prayer in the life of any business cannot be overestimated. Prayer placed at the forefront of a business assures it of receiving God's direction and protection. Prayer for open doors, understanding customer needs, strength to do the task, and abundant business response are some of the common areas for business owners' prayers. Praying in your "secret closet" gives God the opportunity to reveal His wealth building "secrets" to you and publicly display your business success.

But thou, when thou prayest, enter into thy closet, and when thou hast shut thy door, pray to thy Father which is in secret; and thy Father which seeth in secret shall reward thee openly.
                                                        Matthew 6:6 (KJV)

Planning and preparation are vital. Even when you are anointed and gifted, God still honors planning. Planning is important because it prepares you for God's blessing.

   Great planning, great blessing;
   Little planning, little blessing;
   No planning, no blessing.

Commit to the LORD whatever you do, and your plans will succeed.
                                                        Proverbs 16:3 (NIV)

The very idea of developing a plan comes from the nature of God. God is a planner, and since we are created in His image, we have within us the ability to plan and achieve the desires of our hearts.

Wealth Building Secret # 5:
Work will bring God's blessings.

Verses 4 and 5
Prophetic Advice and Coaching:
Pour oil into all the jars, and as each is filled, put it to one side.

The Woman's Response and Follow Through:
They brought the jars to her and she kept pouring.

This principle is always true. However, some believers are waiting for God to drop their blessings from the sky. But, I believe that if God were to miraculously drop blessings from the sky, most people would be too lazy to get up, get dressed, and go outside to pick them up! Remember the advice of a valuable, wealth-producing proverb:

All hard work brings a profit, but mere talk leads only to poverty.
                                             Proverbs 14:23 (NIV)

Wealth Building Secret # 6:
Involve the family or a trusted partner in the plan.

Verses 4 and 5
Prophetic Advice and Coaching:
shut the door behind you and your sons.

The Woman's Response and Follow Through:
She left him and afterward shut the door behind her and her sons.

The sons and mother can now labor together as they work through their grief. They are now brought together for this common cause.

The unity of the new relationship between mother and sons is a great experience for family healing and business success. Unity in human endeavors is found throughout the Scriptures. From the beginning, God said, "It is not good for Adam to be alone." And thus, the unity of mind and muscle becomes the requirement of every human success.

The unity of human mind and muscle is omnipotent. God Himself has said this. When the people of Shinar (Babylonia) in the Old Testament decided to build a city and a temple-tower, a self-worship center, God stopped the project by confusing their language. This, of course, brought division of purpose and a loss of focus that scattered their thoughts and split their original kinship ties. Eventually, this lack of clear uncomplicated communication became man's excuse for tribalism, racism, and hatred of people of other languages and thought patterns. The city they were building was named Babel (that is, BABYL-on).

Even though this human enterprise was started without God's approval, He says that with their unity of mind, mission, and muscle they could do anything they imagined.

The LORD said, "If as one people speaking the same language they have begun to do this, then nothing they plan to do will be impossible for them."
Genesis 11:6 (NIV)

NLT: Nothing will be impossible for them!
NRSV: Nothing that they propose to do will now be impossible for them.

With unity of mind, mission, and muscle, nothing is impossible. We can see these results in the family business enterprise of our new businesswoman.

Wealth Building Secret # 7:
Don't limit yourself.

Verse 6 (NKJV)
When all the jars were full, she said to her son, "Bring me another one." But he replied, "There is not a jar left." Then the oil stopped flowing.

The woman's blessings kept pouring for as many jars as she had previously gathered. What if she had known what God was going to do? Perhaps she would have gathered more jars. Remember, God can do far beyond what you can imagine. Believe Ephesians 3:20 (NKJV): *Now to Him who is able to do exceedingly abundantly above all that we ask or think (NIV: imagine), according to the power that works in us.*

⟳ A KH Quotable Quote ⟲

Don't limit yourself.
Because when you limit yourself, you are limiting God.

Three more principles are in verse seven (NKJV):
Then she came and told the man of God. And he said, "Go, sell the oil and pay your debt; and you and your sons live on the rest."

Wealth Building Secret # 8:
Learn the principles of commerce (buying, selling, and investing).

Verse 7
The prophet said, "Sell." But you say you're not good at selling? Ask the Lord for a special boldness and confidence in presenting what you believe in. Everyone is selling and negotiating all the time. If you don't like the idea of "selling," then merely present, offer, or give an invitation for others to participate.

Did you ask (have to sell) the boss about giving you a raise? As a child, did you ever ask for an ice cream cone, candy, or a new toy? As a teenager, did you ever try to sell your parents on anything? As a parent, have you ever had to sell your child on the virtues of doing something the right way? Your ability to sell or present yourself will directly relate to your overall success in life.

By the way, the single mom in this story could have easily rejected the notion of selling. After all, she was "only a housewife" with no sales experience. Stop your excuses—go sell! You don't need more experience. You already have years of training as a human being. This mother had been selling ideas to her husband and two sons for years.

She was well-qualified to sell a product (a multipurpose olive oil) she knew about and had dealt with all her life. She understood her product's scope, its pricing, the customer needs, and the market distinctives. And she provided a home delivery service! It may have been the first one of its kind in all of Israel. When God gets involved in your business and career, you will get new and innovative ideas about how to run your business, form new products, and service your customers' needs.

You don't need sales experience either. Just believe in the product, believe in God, and believe in the power of God in you. The prophet knew this single mother could sell. He had confidence in her ability. He saw something in her that she had not seen in herself—wealth. What do you see inside of you?

Below, I have listed in modern terms this woman's job qualifications and skills ratings.

The Single Mother's Ten Job Qualifications and Skills
Able Olive Oil Delivery Company, Inc.

JOB QUALIFICATION SKILL	SKILL RATING
1. PRODUCT KNOWLEDGE AND SCOPE OF USAGE Used the multipurpose olive oil product for years, knows of its processing, pricing, usages, shelf life, etc.	EXCELLENT
2. BUSINESS NETWORK Knew the prophets' wives, friends, and neighbors.	EXCELLENT
3. CUSTOMER KNOWLEDGE Intimately knew customer needs and preferences, knew where her perfect customers lived and met socially. She understood women's needs. By the way, if you can understand women's needs and creatively fulfill them, you will never be broke. Women will pay to have their unique needs fulfilled.	EXCELLENT
4. BUSINESS TERRITORY KNOWLEDGE She knew the territory well, having lived there for years.	EXCELLENT
5. PRIOR SALES EXPERIENCE Was always "selling" something to sons and husband, and also occasionally bartering with neighbors and friends.	EXCELLENT

6. MOTIVATION TO CREATE WEALTH   EXCELLENT
   Deep in debt, sons going into slavery.

7. ACCESS TO EMPLOYEES   EXCELLENT
   Utilized her sons in the "family business."

8. MARKET INNOVATION   EXCELLENT
   By understanding the market, she was able to undersell the
   competition. She then was able to innovate and provide a
   home delivery service rather than having the customers come
   to the marketplace. This was a fabulous market innovation,
   and maybe the first in Israel's history.

9. WORK ETHIC LEVEL   EXCELLENT
   She was willing to work hard and ask the neighbors to invest
   in her business idea by loaning her vessels. She showed the
   courage and boldness necessary for business success.

10. LEVEL OF FAITH   EXCELLENT

OVERALL SCORE AND POTENTIAL FOR BUSINESS SUCCESS   EXCELLENT

She had followed the miraculous ministry of Elisha for years. She saw the miracles and believed in the God of Israel. She may not have seen what was inside her, but she trusted the man of God, and even more so, the God of the man. She had faith and was willing to act, which of course, is the only way we know she truly had faith. A life of faith springs into action and brings forth abundance, but a life of fear brings paralyzing immobility and poverty.

You, too, have a long list in your EKG'S Mix (*Experiences, Knowledge, Gifts*, and job qualification *Skills* in that unique mixture of human genius—you). You will bring to any work or endeavor a Unique Personal Touch (UPT) that is patently you.

You have a particular trademark called YOU™. To put a UPT twist upon a popular saying, and it's true: "You will often be imitated, but **never, never** duplicated." As the famed originator of American Jazz, Louis Armstrong once said regarding those who sought to imitate his unique voice and music style, "A lot of cats copy the Mona Lisa, but people still line up to see the original."

Do you believe in what God has given you? Do you really believe? Then, go sell! You can do it. God can do it through you! The buyers are waiting. Those in need are waiting. You've got God's goods and His permission. Go sell!

Wealth Building Secret # 9:
First pay off your debt before you live abundantly.

Verse 7

The prophet knows no matter what the income level, you cannot move up the Wealth Continuum if the debt is greater than the gain. You will still only be at the Poor-2 Level (Upper-Level Poor). So, before the prophet told her to go live abundantly, he first said, "*Pay off your debt.*" Here is that debt reduction issue again. Is God speaking to you about this? Why live above your means? Who are you trying to impress anyway? The Joneses? Your enemies? God? The Devil?

The first law of financial empowerment is to live *below* your means. Do you want to do great things for God? Do you want to change careers? Do you want to move to another city? Do you want to start your own ministry or business?

So, do you need to hear from God regarding your situation? Well then, here's the Word, "*Thus saith the Lord of Wealth, 'Get thee out of debt!*'" [*The Hammonds Book of Abundance*, Chapter 1:9]

Wealth Building Secret # 10:
Now, live abundantly—not irresponsibly.

Verse 7

The prophet then said, "*Live on what is left.*" I hear him saying, "*Go live abundantly. You've suffered financially and emotionally long enough. Congratulations on discovering your inner gifts and utilizing them to become wealthy.*"

This woman made so much money she was propelled up the Wealth Continuum from Level #1 (Destitute) to Level # 6 (Wealthy) in a relatively short period of time. She paid off the debt and had enough in her retirement fund for the family's needs for decades. Wow! Look at God at work through an obedient vessel utilizing her God-given talents to the fullest.

The additional message here is: While you're living in abundance, don't be foolish in the handling of money. Living abundantly does not mean living foolishly or irresponsibly.

BONUS Secret #11:
Never Give Up! There's a Miracle in Persistence

Verse 5 (NKJV)
She left him and afterward shut the door behind her and her sons. They brought the jars to her and she kept pouring.

We are not told how long this business process took. Often events in the Bible that take many months or years are told quickly in a story. The actual longer time period may seem short when told as a story.

Here in our story, though this is a miracle, there is an atmosphere of process. She commissioned her sons to go around to the various parts of Samaria (the province of Elisha's headquarters and probably her residence) and collect the heavy clay pots (vessels) from residents in the area. This suggests time, process, pain, and some disappointments from the people who said "no" or those who thought she was out of her mind. Yet, she perseveres; she persists. God started the flow of oil, but the woman and her sons had to persist in the pouring of the oil.

Are you disappointed because of the length of time God's miracle is taking? As the African American saying goes, "I see it comin', but it's walkin' slow!" Is your miracle "walkin' slow"? Don't stop! It's coming! Keep on collecting those pots by faith and God will reward your faithfulness just as he did the woman in our story. It may be months or years for God's plan to fully come into being. But keep the faith, for God will provide. God *is* providing. We don't know if this miracle process took three weeks, two months, or six months, but it did take time and hard work. After the wait, the woman received the reward for faithful service to God and to her customers.

Nothing is as powerful as persistence. The power of total commitment and persistence to any cause is one of the great wonders of the human nature. As John Calvin Coolidge, thirtieth President of the United States of America, who believed in godliness, prosperity, industry, tenacity, and hard work so eloquently stated:

"Nothing in the world can take the place of persistence. Talent will not; nothing is more common than unsuccessful individuals with talent. Genius will not; unrewarded genius is almost a proverb. Education will not; the world is full of educated derelicts. Persistence and determination alone are omnipotent."

⌘ A Quotable Quote ⌘

Never give in—never, never, never, never. . . .
Never yield to force, never yield to the
apparently overwhelming might of the enemy.
—**Sir Winston Churchill**

Churchill's speech (made on October 29, 1941 during World War II) has been paraphrased into the American tradition this way, "Never give up! Never give up! Never, never, never, never. Never give up!" (Sounds good either way. But, what is it saying to you about your God-given dream?)

Persistence releases the wealth builder within. Purpose and vision (designing a plan) can gestate a miracle, but only a commitment with passion and persistence will bring it forth. Consider the success formula below:

$$(P_1 + P_2) * P_3^2 = \textbf{Prosperity}$$

Success formula explanation:
- Purpose (P_1) and Passion (P_2)
- multiplied by Lots of Persistence (P_3 [P_3 squared = P_3^2])
- produce prosperity.

English translation of the success formula: If you have *purpose* and *passion* with lots of *persistence*, it will produce *prosperity*.

King Solomon, wealthiest man of Israel's ancient history, simply states:

Lazy hands make a man poor, but diligent hands bring wealth.

Proverbs 10:4 (NIV)

Summary of the 10 + 1 Secrets for Producing Wealth

1. *Get out of debt; stay out of debt.*
2. *Use what you have, no matter how small it may seem.*
3. *Go into action; obey God.*
4. *Plan, pray, and prepare in private.*
5. *Work will bring God's blessings.*
6. *Involve the family or a trusted partner in the plan.*
7. *Don't limit yourself.*
8. *Learn the principles of commerce (buying, selling, and investing).*
9. *First pay off your debt before you live abundantly.*
10. *Now—live abundantly.*
11. *Bonus Secret: Never Give Up! There's a Miracle in Persistence.*

The Wealth Builder's Product: Wealth in the Jars

Let's discuss for a moment the value of the product inventory for this woman's oil business. The vessels the prophet was referring to were like the Egyptian and Roman larger amphorae (singular: amphora) vessels used for the transportation of liquids. These clay pots were about three feet high and one foot wide, holding approximately ten to fifteen gallons.

Oil (olive oil) was an essential element of ancient personal and economic life. This oil was extremely multipurpose and was used for food and cooking, anointing the head, anointing the dead, washing the body, fuel for lighting lamps, medicine as a healing agent, trading as a commodity, and in religious ceremony. Kittel's, *Theological Dictionary of the New Testament* says oil is also used in the Bible as a symbol for wealth.

We can get a clearer understanding of the wealth involved here if we use modern economic equivalents for the costs. For example, during OT times, olive oil cost around $84/liter. This is equivalent to around $319/gallon. (We are dealing here with only estimates, not precise figures, but these estimates will give us some indication of the amount of money involved in this lucrative enterprise.)

As I stated above, each amphora held about ten to fifteen gallons. If we use a figure of fifteen gallons per vessel, then the value of each jar *in today's dollars* would be $4,785. Wow, I think I would have collected as many jars as possible! Having been an "expert" in oil and its multi-usage, this woman would certainly have recognized the great value in the jars before her.

So, are you ready for the results? This woman's new business endeavor would only need fifty-three vessels of oil to be valued at more than $250,000 dollars! And, if she took the prophet's hint seriously *"Don't ask for just a few."* (i.e., collect a whole bunch of vessels), she probably gathered many more than that. As a matter of fact, she only needed to collect 209 vessels to have one million dollars in product value.

One day a widow, and a few months later a millionaire! From barely surviving to opulent thriving. Look at God work as *she* worked this little flask of oil into a thriving olive oil empire. God turns a painful economic disaster into a joyful revelation. The God of Wealth reveals to her and to Israel the wealth builder within. Thus, this soon-to-be successful businesswoman begins to discover principles of wealth building that had eluded her for years.

God certainly is a wonder. He takes a mess and makes it a success. He takes the down and turns it around. He takes an economic setback and transforms it into a miracle comeback. Has your comeback come? Be encouraged. If you see it coming, it will arrive.

Now that you've found the secrets, go to it!
GO CREATE SOME WEALTH!

CALCULATING THE VALUE OF THE OLIVE OIL

My calculations for the modern day equivalent of the oil's value are simple. The value of one liter of olive oil during OT times was one denarius. A denarius was equivalent to a day's wages for an average worker. If we use an average USA daily wage of $10.50/hour, then a day's wages would be equivalent to $84.00.

Cost of one liter of olive oil = 1 Denarius = $84
One gallon = 3.8 Liters (rounded off)
Therefore, one gallon = $319 (rounded off) (3.8 liters x $84)
One fifteen gallon amphora vessel = $4,785 (15 x $319)
209 Amphorae Vessels = $1,000,065.00

Personalized Workshops Available

If you wish to get into more personal details regarding the development of the wealth builder within you or those in your group, church, organization, or community, you can arrange a "Creating Wealth God's Way" seminar with Dr. Hammonds. We will come to your church, organization, or community group and present a dynamic workshop featuring the motivation and message of *God Wants You to be Wealthy*.

Dynamic Videos Available

If you want to enjoy a live recording of a Creating God's Way Seminar with three hours of an exciting and uplifting experience, order this motivating video by calling or going to the web site.

For More Information Contact:
    Dr. Kenneth Hammonds
    Spiritual Empowerment, Plus
    P.O. Box 2853 Inglewood, CA 90305-0853
    Phone: 323-753-1366
    Email: KH@WealthyThinking.com
    Coaching Web site: KenHammonds.com

CHAPTER 4

How a Beginner Can Produce Wealth

In this chapter, we will discuss:

✦ The Minimum Wage Mentality
✦ Six Roads to Wealth
✦ A Single Mom with Two Kids Starts a Home-based Business
✦ Considering a Home-based Business
✦ Becoming a Multi-productive Wealth Builder

The Minimum Wage Mentality

Most people suffer from wallet malnutrition.

—**Mark Victor Hansen**

*D*uring a congressional session in the year 2000, the U.S. Congress was in a heated debate about the minimum wage. Most of the Democrats supported a flat and immediate $1.00 an hour increase in the minimum wage, raising it to $6.75 an hour. Most Republicans wanted to increase the $1.00 raise gradually over two years. Without getting into debate about the pros and cons of this $1.00 increase, let me say, it is unfortunate that so many people have a "minimum wage mentality," believing that's the best they can attain. This is the reason why I am so burdened to get the word out about building wealth. Excuse me now, but I must yell at the top of my voice,

STOP THINKING minimum WAGE— THINK MAXIMUM WAGE!

Start to reflect on how you can develop your thinking, your skills, and your resources to make the absolute highest possible income you are able to earn. Never settle for the least, smallest, or minimum. God has placed you at the head, not the tail. That's another way of saying, *God wants you to have the best, not the mess!* God wants you to be out front as a living illustration of His grace and power, not behind at the bottom, as if believing in Him and living for Him will make no difference in a person's life. And you will experience this difference if you follow God's principles as set forth in His Word.

Listen closely to this passage and it's meaning for you:

Deuteronomy 28:12–13, 15, 44, 47 (NIV)
(12) The LORD will open the heavens, the storehouse of his bounty, to

send rain on your land in season and to bless all the work of your hands. You will lend to many nations but will borrow from none.

(13) The LORD will make you the head, not the tail. If you pay attention to the commands of the LORD your God that I give you this day and carefully follow them, you will always be at the top, never at the bottom.

(15) However, if you do not obey the LORD your God and do not carefully follow all his commands and decrees I am giving you today, all these curses will come upon you and overtake you: (44) He [your enemy living with you in your society] will lend to you, but you will not lend to him. He will be the head, but you will be the tail. (47) Because you did not serve the LORD your God joyfully and gladly in the time of prosperity.

Minimum wage thinkers will always be at the mercy of those who control the wage. Minimum wage thinkers settle for the bottom of the wage scale. They settle for the *tail of the wage scale.* But, why settle for the minimum? Why even search for an employer who pays minimum wage? With your $1.00 raise, you can't even get a Big Mac with fries! Besides, when taxes are taken out, your dollar is only about seventy cents anyway.

(Just a note to employers who pay minimum wage: *don't you know that minimum wage means minimum work?*)

So, who exactly are these people called minimum wage thinkers? Minimum wage thinkers are those who *think* and *give* only minimum effort to their endeavors. They consistently do less than their best. These are the chronic underachievers and satisfied C minus students of the world who can and should be doing much better.

Personal Question: Are you a minimum wage thinker making $30,000, $50,000, or $100,000 or more a year? Does your present salary reflect the *best efforts* of your true earning potential? Could you earn two or three times your present income? Are you aiming for the *head of the wage scale?* Stay tuned; this chapter will free your thinking.

I remember one time I was asked to speak for a certain group at a retreat. They asked how much I charged. Being as humble as I am, I told them that I would do it for whatever they had to give (and I didn't say it, but I was thinking that I would have spoken for nothing).

However, in my mind I was actually hoping for at least $50.00. So the organizer said to me, "Well, we have our budget set up for $500.00, is that okay?" Wow! I got offered ten times that which I was prepared for, simply because I didn't ask for minimum. Furthermore, the $500.00 actually had a much higher value. Because of that contact, I developed a contractual relationship that generated hundreds of times my initial "minimum thinking" dollars. Don't limit God. Don't limit yourself. Remember, you CAN produce the wealth you need.

A KH Quotable Quote

*Think $7.00/hour, or think $700.00/hour;
Either way—you're right.*

In this chapter, we will discuss six roads (approaches) available to the beginning wealth builder. These roads range from the simple to the somewhat sophisticated. But, each road is workable for the average person. You only need to find your passion and choose your road. Some of the roads have many streets to choose from and enjoy. Some will require extensive discussion, and others are clear from their descriptions.

The Six Roads to Wealth

Road # 1: KH's emphasis on creating Home-based Businesses
Road # 2: Abraham's system of Multiple Possessions of Wealth
Road # 3: Apostle Paul's system of Tent-making Income
Road # 4: Gorman's system of Multipreneuring
Road # 5: Yates' system of Parallel Careers
Road # 6: Allen's system of Multiple Streams of Income

Road # 1: KH's Home-Based Businesses

A Single Mom with Two Kids Started a Home-based Business

In the previous chapter, we looked at a single mother who took the one thing she had going for her, obeyed God, and received a miracle (2 Kings 4:1–7). Her diligence in working God's plan established her financial future forever. This woman's husband and only means of financial support had died. She and her young sons were devastated. In an effort to get out of the deep debt left to her by her husband, she turned to the prophet Elisha. As a matter of fact, the debt owed by her husband was so overwhelming, the creditors were ready to take her sons into slavery if she didn't pay up.

Since her husband was a member of Elisha's school, she had hoped he or the student prophets would help. She thought Elisha would give her a handout; she left with much more. This single mother came as a beggar but left as a budding entrepreneur and anointed wealth builder.

The challenge from the prophet is the same as the challenge of this chapter: Use your talents, gifts, and resources and go start a home- based business. Go sell! Throughout this chapter, I will give this same challenge to you. Stay tuned. Your financial freedom and the personal expansion of your inner genius may be closer that you think.

In this chapter, I want to make Phase One of P.I.E.S.—Producing Wealth—intensely practical by giving attention to the many roads available to you for generating income. (Remember, P.I.E.S. stands for Producing Wealth, Increasing Wealth, Enjoying Wealth, and Sharing Wealth. This is God's Wealth Cycle. More details about P.I.E.S. in the next chapter.) We will discuss six roads to wealth. We'll focus extensively on home-based businesses (HBB) but also present other roads for building wealth. I trust you'll take in this information personally and actively. And I pray God will place upon you a *wealth builder's anointing*.

A wealth builder's anointing is a divine empowerment, mission, and authority for understanding, producing, and receiving wealth. It also includes a "sixth-sense" business savvy, where an individual recognizes the right avenues, timing, and opportunities for making money and building wealth. An individual with this divine insight will also under-stand how to provide the target market's needs and how to increase busi-ness profitability.

Application of Road # 1 to Your Life

Consider Starting a Home-based Business

How then does a beginner at wealth building start a new life producing wealth? How do you get the wealth builder inside started? Do you quit your job and tell the world, "Here I come"? Not yet. Wait a minute! You'll need some new tools, better building materials, excellent workers, some more experience, and lots of other things before you start working full time on your building. So what's the best way to start? You might say, "Okay, I need some extra income. What do I do? I don't have the time or energy for several jobs." I'm glad you asked that question.

Having several employers is not the answer, but additional sources of income is. Have you considered a home-based business (HBB)? A HBB is one that you run from somewhere in your house or apartment. You may perform your service in the home or you may perform your service outside the home. The key is that you are not renting office space outside your home to do your business.

Part of changing your belief system to maximum wage thinking is realizing you *can* produce and create finances and build wealth in your life. The first thing to remember is—do not immediately quit your day job to start your own full-scale, debt-ridden business. You must look into yourself, searching for the one talent, gift, or ability you have, or the thing you are most interested in, and start a nice little HBB. Later, you may expand the business or start a new full-blown business with employees, common stock, buildings, and the like. But for now, let's get going gradually and peep before we leap.

The probabilities for starting, maintaining, and doing well in an HBB are great. It is possible, especially for those of you who believe you aren't talented. With the great changes to modern communications like fax machines, cell phones, pagers, voice mail, the Internet, computers, email, and other technologies, the "little guy" and part timer can look and feel as professional as the large corporations.

Great Information in Books

Go to your local library or bookstore and look in the section for books on starting small businesses or HBBs. I recently saw over fifty titles in a bookstore. One resource I saw listed over 500 small businesses you could start. Another was called *The Home Business and Small Business Answer Book* (2nd edition), by Janet Attard. It is a valuable resource. It has all the questions you could possibly ask, and the answers.

Other books focused particularly on the small businesses and HBBs that you could start for under $1,000. Some of the multilevel marketing programs require $300 dollars or less. Some moneymaking ideas require no more than what you already have "in your house"—like baking, writing, speaking, babysitting, etc. See the *Wealthy Resources* section at the end of the book for more resources.

Baking for Dollars

In my Sunday morning Bible study, called "*God's Principles of Abundance*" (GPA), a retired great grandmother asked, "What can I do to help my church raise funds for the building of the new cathedral?" She first thought she had nothing to give or offer in her retirement age. However, in one class session when we were discussing the 2 Kings Chapter 4 passage, she realized she could bake cakes—and she did and was able to raise over $1,000 for her church. Anyone can generate money, if they just look inside.

By the way, don't discredit the idea of making a lot of money by baking. Just consider Famous Amos or Mrs. Field's Cookies. Millions of dollars are made by people just like you who only have *one* talent or skill. Now you know that's all you need! Perhaps the only difference between you and them is their huge compelling drive to succeed. Do you have a compelling drive to succeed and create wealth? Whether caused by pain, passion, purpose, or profit, it is this burning drive that brings success to any endeavor.

Get by with a Little Help from Your Friends

Have you found yourself $20,000 or more in debt? Why not become a wealth builder instead of a wealth destroyer? (Credit card debt destroys your hard earned wealth.) Why not create some wealth and use it to eliminate your debt? If you can't think of anything by yourself, do some brainstorming with your friends (only your positive ones). Have four or five over for dinner or just for a visit. After dinner, have a brainstorming session for eliminating your debt. Listen to them talk about your talents and what kinds of things you could do to eliminate the debt. Can you type, create t-shirts, speak at events, or run an e-based business on the Internet?

I don't know if all your friends' suggestions will be great ones, but I can tell you this: It will start your mind moving and you will gain valuable ideas. Best of all, it will help you get the confidence to pull it off. You can do so many things.

Over sixty HBBs are mentioned in the next section. You would be surprised how your creativity will rise to the surface when you utilize all the EKG'S (Experience, Knowledge, Gifts, and Skills) within you.

Get Your Own Wealth
Why not consider building some wealth for yourself so you can enjoy life and provide for your loved ones and the organizations you want to support? Why sit around and wait for Congress to give you a dollar?

Furthermore, if we consider our downsizing frenzy, when Congress does get you that dollar, the employer may lay you off anyway. Many small businesses can't absorb rising employee costs, and the larger firms may lay you off because the stockholders want to see a better profit from the business. Stop this nonsense and make some wealth on your own. Do it now—while you still have your day job.

Many Who Make $100,000 + a Year Still Have No Job Security

This potential for job loss is no different for the bigger wage earner. In fact, the higher paying positions may actually be *more* susceptible to elimination than the minimum wage positions. Just miss one social event with an important client, and you may be picking up your last paycheck at the end of the week! In today's employment climate, unless workers or managers are directly responsible for creating company revenues, they are subject to all the whims of restructuring or downsizing—just like the minimum wage earners.

A Listing of Over Sixty Home-based Businesses

So many possibilities are available for developing businesses right from your home. These are also called Small Office Home Office (SOHO) businesses. Even if you think none of the things mentioned here are for you, this list will at least stir your mind about other ventures for which you may be best suited. Most of these can be done part time, and all from your home. With an HBB, you start small and proceed at your own pace. You don't risk your life's savings trying to buy a franchise or existing business. And you don't have to beg your boss for a raise or threaten a strike to get $1.00 more an hour.

After reading the HBBs on the next page, come back to this sheet and fill in the various HBBs that appeal to you. If the one(s) you have in mind aren't listed, just place them here. As you think on your final three, thoughtfully consider which will be your top choice. Get ready. Prepare for some new excitement in your life if you wish to spread your wings. Move cautiously, but enjoy the business and enjoy your life of creating wealth.

YOUR TOP CHOICES OF INTEREST FOR HBBS

Top Ten Choices	Top Five Choices	Top Three Choices	Top Choice
_____			
_____			
_____	_____		
_____	_____	_____	
_____	_____	_____	_____
_____	_____	_____	
_____	_____		
_____			
_____			
_____			

SPECIAL EVENTS
children's party planner
tutoring
kids taxi service
disk jockey
wedding services
part-time musician

HUMAN SERVICES
senior care
child care
baby sitting

HOME SERVICES
handyman
interior designer
carpet cleaning
house painter
maid service
organizer (closets,
    desks, rooms)
home inspector for real
    estate companies

PERSONAL SERVICES
personal trainer
cruise travel agent
translator
image consultant
beauty consultant
voice coach

**BUSINESS-TO-
BUSINESS SERVICES**
business consultant
career coach
personal coach
business support services
employee trainer
résumé writer
business plan writer

COMPUTER SERVICES
computer repair
computer training
internet trainer
Web designer
graphic designer

GARDENING SERVICES
landscaping
plant care
lawn care

ARTS AND CRAFTS
gift baskets
making greeting cards
making jewelry
sewing

PET SERVICES
dog training
dog walking
dog grooming

FOOD SERVICES
catering
baking (cakes, pies,
    cookies, etc.)
nutrition consultant

MISCELLANEOUS
paralegal
tax preparation
proofreader
gift wrapper
seminar speaker
seminar promoter
freelance writer
network marketing
    (*Beware: many are
    too good to be true.*)
automobile detailing
private investigator

Choosing an additional source of income can be overwhelming if you read the list and try to choose something on the basis of only making money. However, as you consider the above or those business ideas now coming to your mind, remember to set the stage by thinking about hobbies, interests, or skills you already have. Don't just work for money. How boring!

These Seven P's Will Assist You in Starting

✦ PRAY.

✦ Look for POSSIBILITIES.

✦ Where is your PASSION?

✦ Is there financial PROFIT in it?

✦ Is this something you can do now in the PRESENT? (Not something that will take years to get going.)

✦ PREPARE yourself through research before starting.

✦ Once you get started, PERSIST.

A Special Note for Mothers at Home: An organization called Work At Home Moms has a resourceful Web site, WAHM.com and a book entitled *Work At Home Moms* by Cheryl Demos, from Hazen Publishers.

You Need a Metanoia to Move Forward

Metanoia (meta-NOI-a) is a Greek word that means *a radical change in thinking; a shift in attitude.* A metanoia for your life means changing from poverty thinking and awakening to start a new life. This word describes the essence of why I have written *God Wants You to be Wealthy.* I want you to get a metanoia of who you are and what you can do. A radical change in your thinking and attitude will bring a radical change in your behavior and in your life.

Have you checked your attitude lately? Many people need some assistance in this area. Some people know they have a bad attitude and they want everyone else to know it, too. Are you still mad that he left you with the kids and the bills? "That no good so and so . . ." Or maybe you are angry that she divorced you and is taking all your money and your children.

Yes, people are angry about so much and it causes them to have a bad attitude. I have a word from the Lord for you: *get a metanoia!*

Stop blaming God, him, her, them, those people, that racial group, those women, those men, your kids, your arthritis, your physical appearance, or your whatever. You are so much greater than complaints. God can't work through a murmurer (a complainer). Get an attitude of gratitude and release the grudge. You will actually feel better and live longer.

Do all things without murmurings and disputings.

Philippians 2:14 (KJV)

In everything you do, stay away from complaining and arguing.

Philippians 2:14 (NLT)

Stop! Place your life's remote control on pause. You don't need to walk around with a big chip on your shoulder. You are the person who can decide how you will feel. The woman of 2 Kings Chapter 4 could have spent her time complaining to the prophet about her husband. She could have kept the grudge for several years and spent her energy telling others about how her "no good husband" left her in debt with two kids.

But instead, she got to work and turned a negative into a positive. Just think, if her husband had never died and left her in debt she would have never experienced the miracle of the wealth within her own hands. You would be surprised how using your talent, working, and doing good can help relieve bitterness and release positive energy.

Don't let the bitterness of your past destroy the beauty of your future. Get a new metanoia. Change your attitude and change your life! In the NT, *metanoia* is generally translated into English by the word *repent*. That's exactly what some of us need to do. "Lord I repent. I need a new attitude. I don't like being angry and upset. I'm going to look to You and celebrate what You've given me."

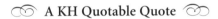

A KH Quotable Quote

*Don't let the bitterness of your past
destroy the beauty of your future.*

But, just how does metanoia relate to starting an HBB? To properly implement an HBB, you must have a shift in thinking. You need a metanoia. You think differently when you are working for yourself.

The **first metanoia** is to know you are self-employed already and that your employer, Company XYZ, is merely one of your clients. Believe me, your boss, no matter how much he or she likes you, only considers you an employee. Although the boss calls you "family," you are only part of the employee family. When you are no longer an employee, you are no longer part of the family. Remember, the decision to be an employee is primarily the employer's choice, not yours. They decide to hire, and they decide to fire—as they desire.

The **second metanoia** is to know you must have multiple avenues of wealth production. It's the only way you can start to have financial wealth and freedom. Remember, most employers are not trying to pay you the maximum salary they can. They want to pay you the minimum. I must say here, I am not in the least bashing employers. I'm only stating the reality that most of you try to avoid thinking about. The employer must make a profit and the most expensive component of your employer's business is you (employee costs). To your employer, you are an economic cost unit. Face the truth: if your employer could get along without you, he or she would.

I can see the employer's viewpoint and, if you were honest, you would see it, too. You think your employer owes you a raise because you've hung around for another year. You think your employer must pay you "what you are worth." For most employers you are a *consumer* of profit not a *producer* of profit. That's why sales people get paid more than office people. Sales people produce wealth for the company.

Why am I saying all of this? What does this have to do with you? Well, in a nutshell, I'm saying: don't totally depend on one source of income. When that well dries up, where will you go for more water?

Become a Multi-productive Creator of Wealth

The above leads me to a discussion of the benefits of having many avenues of wealth production called Multiple Streams of Income (MSI).

Road # 2: Abraham's
Multiple Possessions of Wealth

A Biblical Example: Abraham, the Father of Faith, Tithing, and Wealth

Abraham had wealth: a large diversified portfolio of multiple possessions. As we have stated before, he's the first person in the Bible to be called *rich* or *wealthy*. Abraham is the father of wealth. He is the father of faith, tithing, and wealth.

Abram was very rich [NIV: very wealthy] in livestock, in silver, and in gold.
Genesis 13:2 (NKJV)

The LORD has blessed my master greatly, and he has become great; and He has given him flocks [sheep and/or goats] and herds [cattle], silver and gold, male and female servants, and camels and donkeys.
Genesis 24:35 (NKJV)

Abraham's Diversified Wealthy Portfolio Included:

- ✦ Livestock, food, and commodities for trade (sheep and/or goats and cattle)
- ✦ Money (silver and gold)
- ✦ Employees (male and female workers/servants)
- ✦ Transportation (camels and donkeys)
- ✦ Land (mentioned in Genesis 12:1)

As a multi-productive wealth builder, Abraham enjoyed the flow of many rivers of wealth.

A Modern Example: Al and Hattie Hollingsworth

For those of you with the gift and tenacity for starting a full-blown business, here is an example of some modern day Abrahamic multi-producers—Al and Hattie Hollingsworth. The Hollingsworth couple came from the grip of bankruptcy to establish and operate a multi-million dollar contract packaging business called Aldelano Corporation, whose clients include Kellogg, Proctor and Gamble, and General Mills. The company has major plants and offices in Michigan, Ohio, Tennessee, and California. Aldelano Packaging product lines include bags, boxes, cartons, pouches, and other packages used for food, health, beauty aids, household cleaning products, hardware, toys, and liquids and solids.

This business was built with Mr. Hollingsworth's God-given business skill and prayer. Mrs. Hattie Hollingsworth is an accomplished Christian recording artist and songwriter, as well as a professional interior designer. Both, as African Americans, have never let anyone or any system stand in the way of vigorously pursuing their business ventures.

The Hollingsworths have also moved into other areas of Christian ministry, including adult and youth training in entrepreneurship, a recording studio, producing and selling books and tapes, and developing and managing the beautiful Alhatti Christian Resort in Idyllwild, California. When you are Abrahamic in your wealth building, you can do so much more for others.

You, too, must become a multi-productive creator of wealth and have multi-flowing rivers of income. I know many of you think you have no time for producing additional income and that your employer is treating you fine. However, remember the revolutionary concept that I just mentioned in the last section: you are not an employee; you are self-employed.

Your task in your employment life is to produce income. Staying employed with a particular company is only *one* of the many ways at your disposal for producing income. If you had income properties generating $200,000 a year profit, you would probably not consider working for your employer at all!

Application of Road # 2 to Your Life

The primary application you can glean from Abraham's life is that he is both a man of faith and a man of wealth. It's okay to be wealthy. As a matter of fact, it's better to be wealthy and have God than to be wealthy without God, because without God you're not wealthy at all.

Abraham inspires all of us to look at possessions in a new way. It's all right for you to have possessions; your possessions, however, should not have you. We can also see in Abraham a man who believed God. He is a diligent worker and knew the value of having multiple possessions and a workforce for maintaining his wealth.

The Father of Wealth teaches us that faith and wealth are not incompatible. In fact, they are necessary to performing the task God has called us to.

Road # 3: Apostle Paul's Tent-making Income

Even a spiritual giant like the apostle Paul made tents "on the side." Church work was not his only source of income. Many bi-vocational pastors, people in the music industry, people in the entertainment industry, and other bi-vocational career people can identify with this Pauline model. Although I suppose Paul's situation could more exactly be called both a bi-vocational career and a road-based business instead of a home-based business. He made his tents while traveling around preaching the gospel and setting up churches. This is a beginning step on the road to wealth and an important one if you are presently involved in ministry.

Application of Road # 3 to Your Life

Paul's example reminds those in transition from part-time ministry service to full-time ministry service that it is acceptable to work in "secular" employment. Of course, today, Christian Life expositors warn us about referring to any part of our lives as secular. Secular means without any reference or consideration of God or spiritual things. That is, of course, impossible for the Christian. For the spiritually minded, all of life's experiences and activities are to be sacred and holy before God.

So, if you are in ministry transition or if things have gotten rough after you went into full-time ministry, it's okay to get a job. It is not acceptable to expect others to support you when you will not provide for yourself and become a burden to the ministry. Also, it makes for a happier marriage when your spouse does not have to work hard to support you because you are only going to do *ministry* and not work that *secular stuff*. The day may come, and it will if that's your desire, but until it does—get a job! You can then go from full-time outside the job to part-time at the job; then from part time in the ministry to full time in the ministry.

Paul reminds us of the sacredness of working with one's hands. God specially designed the human hands for the work of production and creation. They were also intended to display your genius and ability in shaping your own future. Human hands make or shape a physical expression of God's invisible presence within. So, if you are not now employed or need additional employment, Paul shows the value of such work so as not to burden a struggling ministry with financial obligations.

In the name of the Lord Jesus Christ, we command you, brothers, to keep away from every brother who is idle and does not live according to the teaching you received from us. For you yourselves know how you ought to follow our example. We were not idle when we were with you, nor did we eat anyone's food without paying for it. On the contrary, we worked night and day, laboring and toiling so that we would not be a burden to any of you. We did this, not because we do not have the right to such help, but in order to make ourselves a model for you to follow. For even when we were with you, we gave you this rule: "If a man will not work, he shall not eat."

2 Thessalonians (3:6–10 NIV)

I have not coveted anyone's silver or gold or clothing. You yourselves know that these hands of mine have supplied my own needs and the needs of my companions. In everything I did, I showed you that by this kind of hard work we must help the weak, remembering the words the Lord Jesus himself said: 'It is more blessed to give than to receive.'"

Acts 20:33–35 (NIV)

Three Modern Approaches to Personal Multi-productivity

Three authors have written creatively on the subject of personal multi-productivity. These creative income-producing concepts are important for your employment life as a wealth builder. They are: *multipreneuring, parallel careers, and multiple streams of income.* I'm sure you'll appreciate the emphasis of each approach.

Road # 4: Gorman's Multipreneuring

In his interesting book, *Multipreneuring: How to Prosper in the Emerging Freelance Economy*, Tom Gorman calls his view of becoming a multi-productive wealth person *multipreneuring*. He defines multipreneuring as a career strategy in which we use every skill we have to develop and build multiple careers for ourselves. This idea of multipreneuring is being utilized by other authors to mean the general concept of the one becoming the many—that is to say, using your one talent, skill, or idea so that it can result in many different sources of income. Do you have at least one skill? If you do (and I'm sure you do), then you can also have many sources of income.

Application of Road # 4 to Your Life

From Gorman's approach, you will go far with only a little. This approach is perfect for those of you who believe you only have one talent, or one means, of generating income. Gorman's road is for the shy among us who can't seem to consider themselves as great or as multitalented. It's the road for everyday folks who want to work intelligently.

Think of your *one* EKG'S (experience, gift, talent, or skill) as a seed. From one apple seed comes the tree's bark, roots, limbs, and fruit. I've got a question for you: How many apples are in one apple seed? One, fifteen, fifty, one hundred, one thousand, ten thousand, one million, Well, you don't know, do you? The answer, of course, is infinite. There is no way to precisely calculate it.

The mathematical potential of the production from just one apple tree is astonishing. One apple tree can live as long as 200 years, and in each season, it can produce as many as 2,000 apples. So, in the 200-year cycle of an apple tree, it can produce over 400,000 apples and over two million seeds (with just five seeds in each apple). If these figures are multiplied out to just the second generation (two million times two million), one 200-year apple tree has the potential of producing at least 4 trillion trees! So, I suppose the answer to my original question which was, "How many apples are in one apple seed?" is _____. (Still infinite.)

So, the next time you look at an apple seed, know that you're looking at a powerful entity. Never devalue the immense power of a single seed. And likewise, never devalue the immense financial potential and power of a single EKG'S. That experience, which was so bad at the time, may add a UPT (Unique Personal Touch) to your life that brings you success. And if you are able to present that "bad" experience to an interested audience and creatively market it in the form of a seminar, book, CD, or DVD, you may even produce great financial income and notoriety. Indeed, people will pay you well to tell, or write, your "rags to riches," your "sad to glad," or your "down and under to overcomer" story.

The Scriptures understand this concept of small to large perfectly. Zechariah the prophet was well qualified to motivate Israel to finish the temple-rebuilding project. Even though they had only completed a seemingly insignificant foundation, this prophet of the Spirit encouraged them to appreciate the small beginning of the future magnificent temple. He states a basic principle of human potential and progress in his statement, encouraging the people "not to despise the day of the small things" (Zachariah 4:10).

The Hebrew word here for *despised* is related to an Arabic root that means to *lift one's head high in the air with disrespect.* Don't *dis* the seed (disregard, disgrace, discourage, or despise), for when the seed is properly nurtured, there will come a day of rejoicing when the small seed matures into a full-grown blessing.

One Book, One Million

Your one EKG'S is just like that. You can reap money for years by just fully developing a single product. For example, let's say you will write a book. (I'm sure you can. 82 percent of people in the USA say they have at least one book in them. Is it in *you*?) From that one book, you cannot only sell copies of the book, but have seminars, workshops, and make presentations at schools, civic groups, and churches. You can then produce other products like CD's, audio tapes, video tapes, and many other things.

These are exactly the kinds of things that I'll be doing with this one book! As a matter of fact, I have formulated more than twenty-one multi-dimensions from this one book!

Note: For those of you who would be interested in writing and marketing your book in this new way, stay tuned to my Web site, *KenHammonds.com*, or call me for more information about live classes, teleclasses, and workshops on writing and marketing your great book idea.

One good book idea is worth millions of dollars. Millionaire maker and trainer Robert Allen documents that he has made over 200 million dollars from just one book with a real estate concept called *nothing down*. Want even more shock? Listen to this quote from his book *Multiple Streams of Income:* "During my lifetime, over $1 billion is going to be dug out of the mine shaft called *Nothing Down* real estate. It was a *billion-dollar idea!*"

So, no more excuses! Successfully implementing Gorman's multi-preneuring approach will change your life in a dramatic way. What million-dollar idea is floating around in your creative brain right now?

Road # 5: Yates' Parallel Careers

Martin Yates, in his book, *Beat the Odds*, has an interesting approach to multi-productivity. He proposes a solution called *parallel careers*. Yates believes all of us should be pursuing a path of three careers **at the same time**: *core career, entrepreneurial career, and dream career.*

The *core career* is vital for your income and the main part of your career life. However, the *entrepreneurial career* gives you more personal freedom and helps you develop relationships outside the core career. It gives the financial autonomy necessary in these times. *Dream careers* are hobbies or interests you do just for the joy of doing them and having a fulfilling life. Actually, your dream career can help you develop the other career opportunities and may in time become a source of income in its own right.

Yates further states:

Core career is for life: putting food on the table and meeting the basics needs of life.

Entrepreneurial career is for liberty: the freedom to develop your gifts
   fully without outside constraints.
Dream career is for the pursuit of happiness: fulfilling the passion of
   your life.

I think I've heard this somewhere before: life, liberty, and the pursuit of
happiness. Oh yes, just in case you've forgotten, it's in the Declaration
of Independence, written by Thomas Jefferson, July 4, 1776, for the 13
British colonies that later became the United States of America.

The second sentence of the Declaration reads: "We hold these truths
to be self-evident, that all men are created equal, that they are endowed
by their Creator with certain unalienable Rights, that among these are
Life, Liberty, and the pursuit of Happiness."

How about that? Pursuing parallel careers is a self-evident right of
humanity! Enjoy your freedom and the pursuit of your dreams. Express
yourself and your occupational calling through your parallel careers.

Another Modern Example: George B. Thompson

One of my former success students and now colleague, Mr. George B.
Thompson, is a living example of what a metanoia and application of the
above multi-productive avenues can do for a career and a life. George
had a well-paying job selling 401k retirement plans for a living.

However, he actually wanted to be employed by using his natural
financial understanding and talents as a full-service financial planner
and broker of financial instruments. George was enrolled in my School
of Success (SOS) program. In one of the sessions, I was discussing multipreneuring and parallel careers. George quickly understood the principles and how they applied to him. He immediately got a sales job using
his talents and began to increase his income and knowledge base.

George then began to give back to the community and founded
Millionaires in Training (MIT) and Young MIT's. His goal is to assist
people in becoming debt free and financially free. George has been debt
free for several years. (Actually, I wonder if he has ever been in debt!) He
now has a job with a large financial firm applying his natural talents
managing millions of dollars in financial investments. In addition to

this, he is still expanding his God-given public presentation skills through books, tapes, and television appearances. (His book, *Millionaires in Training*, is mentioned in the *Wealthy Resources* section of this book.)

As a full-service financial planner, he now earns three times what he earned only three years ago. George is not yet through; he now has short-term goals that include saving all the income from one stream and living on the other streams. Triple your income in three years? Save one source of income and live off the rest? Impossible? No! A mindset of multi-productivity can accomplish great things for those who follow where their talents lead and are persistent as their dreams unfold.

Application of Road # 5 to Your Life

Yates' road is a good approach for those of you who are security oriented. You don't like just jumping out there. You want to understand what's going on and how you can gradually begin to build your wealth. You like working at your job and you feel somewhat fulfilled. However, you do know that as far as your employer is concerned, they may need to someday downsize and the down part is you! You can now begin to take more control of your career and financial future. Remember, your goal in your career and economic life is to stay employed and financially abundant, not necessarily to stay with one employer.

Yates' road is exciting and extremely workable. It's the perfect approach also for those of you who feel you've got many EKG'S. You know you are multi-talented and have much on the ball. Yates' approach takes a lot of energy, talent, and scheduling to run these three parallel careers in your life. But, if you can effectively do it, you'll never be broke again and you'll always be moving forward along your chosen career path or paths yet to be discovered.

Through this road, you are always discovering and developing your talents in different areas. You've heard that "variety is the spice of life." With Yates, variety multiplies the money of life. Think on and plan for the entrepreneurial career you can start. Or, start to volunteer for that dream career you've always felt a special calling toward. Traveling the road of parallel careers is an exciting one aimed at developing your talents and stretching the borders you've placed upon the development of your wealth potential.

Road # 6: Allen's Multiple Streams of Income (MSI)

In his book, *Multiple Streams of Income: How to Generate a Lifetime of Unlimited Wealth,* real estate wealth guru Robert Allen lays out a comprehensive and detailed approach to personal multi-productivity. Allen makes an interesting point that in the 1950s it only took one stream of income for a family to survive. Today, few families can survive on less than two streams of income, and in the future, those two streams won't be enough.

So, his book lays out a series of ten possible streams of income. Before you think of these as ten "jobs," consider that he is describing residual income, investment income, rental income, and the Internet income strategies as some of the ways to have multiple streams of income. These are splendid ways to produce income over and over while having done the initial hard work only at the beginning (passive income).

It's an excellent book and has good, workable plans. Allen likes to divide his MSI system into four major ways for creating wealth. He calls them *money mountains.* The four money mountains are real estate, investments, marketing, and the Internet.

Robert Allen's Multiple Streams of Income

Real Estate
1. Basic buying and holding of real estate properties
2. Foreclosures and flippers
3. Tax lien certificates

Investments
4. Basic stock market investments through index funds
5. Accelerated stock market strategies
6. Stocks options

Marketing
7. Network marketing
8. Infopreneuring (selling information and expertise)
9. Licensing your information

The Internet
10. Using various Internet strategies (email, Web site sales, etc.)

Robert Allen has also written another bestselling book entitled *Multiple Streams of Internet Income: How Ordinary People Make Extraordinary Money Online*. In this book, he speaks of powerful yet simple strategies for Internet success and the many ways to make money on the Internet. Some of these include opening your own bookstore, joining affiliate programs, and selling your own products and services online. He discusses advertisement, how to build a profitable Web site, and how to make money with email newsletters.

Application of Road # 6 to Your Life

The strength of the Robert Allen road is the joy of knowing that you are developing several avenues, or streams, of income. Also, Allen stresses the need to create residual income streams that keep on producing long after you have initially started them. And when you learn from Allen, you have one of the best mentors in the world. Allen, with his *nothing down* real estate approach and his new MSI approach, has perhaps helped to make more millionaires than anyone else on Earth.

With his approach, you can choose a major money-making mountain and a minor money-making approach for residual income. In his book, Allen walks you right through the steps for each mountain. Certainly, anyone can create income from the wealth of any or all of these mountains.

Find a mountain and climb it! Keep your day job and climb a mountain as a part timer. It's up to you. It depends upon how fast you want to climb and how much wealth you want to mine from the riches buried deep within each mountain.

Conclusion

So, whether it's taking the journey of:
Road # 1: KH's Home-based Businesses
Road # 2: Abraham's Multiple Possessions of Wealth

Road # 3: Apostle Paul's Tent-Making Income
Road # 4: Gorman's Multipreneuring
Road # 5: Yates' Parallel Careers
Road # 6: Allen's Multiple Streams of Income

. . . they all agree that what I'm calling *a multi-productive wealth flow* is an important element in building and maintaining wealth.

By now, I hope you have rid your consciousness of the minimum wage mentality and are convinced that you *can* become a multi-productive wealth builder. This is the need of the present and the wave of the future. It is as old as Abraham and as spiritual as Paul. So pray, study, and find your primary road. You may get ideas from all of them, but you'll need focus to be successful.

If you don't know where to start, visit my Web site at *KenHammonds.com,* and look for classes and workshops. Or, give me a call at 323-753-1366 about other opportunities to discover and release the wealth builder within.

CHAPTER 5

God's Wealth Cycle: P.I.E.S.

**The Four-fold, God-ordained
Cycle of True Wealth**

In this chapter, we will discuss:

✦ **P.I.E.S.: A New Discovery**
✦ **Introducing the P.I.E.S. Wealth Cycle**
✦ **Tithing: A Wealth-building Strategy?**

My New Discovery: P.I.E.S.

∽ A KH Quotable Quote ∾

*All the problems of the world are caused by poverty
(lack of spiritual or material wealth). And poverty brings despair;
but God's Wealth Cycle brings wealth and hope.*

t is my joy to announce I
have discovered a power-
ful wealth cycle. This discovery has
been developing over a number of
years and finally fully formed only
after my long and careful reflection
upon various human societies,
conditions, and systems.

This discovery was sparked by
my wondering why some individuals, communities, and nations were
economically successful and others
were burdened with poverty and
failure. By observing economically
successful individuals and human

| **Phase One**
Producing Wealth
(creating/generating) |
| **Phase Two**
Increasing Wealth
(preserving/investing) |
| **Phase Three**
Enjoying Wealth
(living/celebrating) |
| **Phase Four**
Sharing Wealth
(caring for/empowering others) |

systems (successful families, organizations, societies, and governments),
I was able to arrive step by step to the wealth cycle.

Of course, the cycle has been there for ages. It was practiced in past
centuries and is still practiced today by successful individuals and systems. It is my observation that individuals and systems practicing the
wealth cycle become wealthy and successful. They are able to advance
along the Wealth Continuum. (Refer back to Chapter 3, or see Appendix
Four for more about the continuum.) Those who do not activate the
wealth cycle are unable to reach the level of success and wealth for which
they have the potential. Indeed, for those who ignore the cycle, there is
usually, and unfortunately, more poverty and pain than wealth.

My "discovery," therefore, is not so much that a cycle exists, but in presenting the cycle in a unique four-fold model. This universal wealth cycle has four phases: Phase One: Producing Wealth; Phase Two: Increasing Wealth; Phase Three: Enjoying Wealth; and Phase Four: Sharing Wealth. The first letter of each of these phases is where I get the acrostic, P.I.E.S. God wants all humanity to produce, increase, enjoy, and share its wealth.

If followed, this Divine Cycle will help individuals reach new personal levels of empowerment, and at the same time raise societies to new levels of productivity. Actualization of economic potentiality can now, under this wealth cycle, become a theme and the experience for every individual and social group. In the P.I.E.S. system, each element in the flow of the cycle of wealth is important to God's plan for wealthy human existence.

PIES for Everyone

Economist Dr. Paul Zane Pilzer has a view of prosperity called *economic alchemy*. This view says "Don't just cut up the little American Prosperity Pie—make a bigger pie."

Dr. Pilzer's economic alchemy view is the belief that there is room enough for all of us to prosper. Scientific alchemy was originally the practice of early chemists in Medieval times who wanted to turn lead and other metals into gold, discover a universal cure for disease, and discover the means for prolonging life. Pilzer uses the word alchemy in the secondary sense: the process of transforming something common into something precious.

Dr. Pilzer says the alchemist scientists of an earlier era firmly believed, "God would not put us on earth in a scarce environment, where only I can get rich by taking from you. He would give me *a way that we both can get wealthy* [emphasis mine], which is what our whole modern society and advancing technology is all about." [*Power CD, Anthony Robbins Interviews Paul Zane Pilzer, Part I.* 1994 by ZCI Publishing, Inc. Page 61.]

Pilzer believes we have an unlimited supply of resources within the Earth and within ourselves to do the things we need to do. Advancing technology gives us the ability to utilize Earth's resources in a new way. With this technology, the Earth's seeming scarce resources can be prudently utilized to produce abundance.

Pilzer goes on to say, "An economist, I say, takes things and moves them around. Takes a pie and says, 'Here's how you slice it better.' An economic alchemist says, 'Throw away the knife; let's bake a bigger pie [so] that everybody can have a piece.'"

That's my view—plus some. I say, let's expand human innovation and potential "to the max." Let's show people how to make different kinds of prosperity pies for themselves and others. Let's make PIES for everyone! This chapter introduces and discusses each phase of the P.I.E.S. cycle. Embracing God's Wealth Cycle will release God's wealth flow to the world. However, ignoring, breaking, or destroying God's Wealth Cycle will limit the flow of wealth from God to humankind.

Introducing the P.I.E.S. Wealth Cycle

Phase One
P: Producing Wealth

The Scriptural Command
to Produce

God's original intent for humans was for them to be entrepreneurial and produce whatever they needed for existing and prospering on this Earth. God has wisely placed within humanity an urge—a compelling desire to produce, progress, and be successful.

Phase One **Producing Wealth** (creating/generating)
Phase Two **Increasing Wealth** (preserving/investing)
Phase Three **Enjoying Wealth** (living/celebrating)
Phase Four **Sharing Wealth** (caring for/empowering others)

Humans (Adam, Eve, and their children) were given an original mandate by God in the Genesis 1:28 directive to "be fruitful and multiply" (produce abundantly, produce wealth). The God-given mental abilities, talents, and gifts resident in humanity also mandate this. We are **obligated** to produce wealth in order to enjoy being fully human. Entrepreneurship (creative productivity), therefore, is at the very heart of what it means to be human.

Humans as Producers of Wealth

First of all, the ability to produce with infinite variety is resident only in humanity and humanity's gifts as given by God. Humans have shown this ability from cavemen to city dwellers.

Phase One: Producing Wealth, is the starting place for wealth within the individual and society. Here is the good news: God has placed within human beings the priceless ability to produce wealth. The ability to produce wealth is more important than possessing wealth. The man who possesses wealth but is unable to produce more will soon discover poverty. He will find he has not only lost his wealth, but even more tragically, he is unable to replace it.

Yes, you can produce wealth. It is a distinctly human ability given by God. Therefore, since you are human, try it out! You'll like it.

The Wealth Cycle: An Unfolding Revelation of Scripture

And you shall remember the LORD your God, for it is He who gives you power to get wealth, that He may establish His covenant which He swore to your fathers, as it is this day.

Deuteronomy 8:18 (NKJV)

But remember the LORD your God, for it is he who gives you the ability to produce wealth, and so confirms his covenant, which he swore to your forefathers, as it is today.

Deuteronomy 8:18 (NIV)

My progressive understanding of this powerful Scripture in Deuteronomy 8:18 sparked the discovery of the first phase of the wealth cycle.

Here is the progressive nature of the discovery.

First, there was the discovery of Deuteronomy 8:18 in the King James Version. The phrase in the KJV reads, "power to get wealth." That is a strong phrase, but the translation seems to hint that you can get wealth from "out there somewhere."

The next phase of my revelation came from the eye-opening translation of the New International Version. It places emphasis on the power within the individual. It reads, "the ability to produce wealth." In this context, the Hebrew word for "ability" refers to ability or power conferred or bestowed by God. In the OT it is used of prophetic power and here of God's wealth producing power. Indeed, I hear God saying, "I have bestowed upon you, MY ability to produce wealth." God's ability works through our availability. Just think about it. You have the God-given ability to produce wealth. Wealth is not merely "out there somewhere," waiting for you to stumble across it by accident or luck. Your wealth comes from within, the human power within. It is an empowerment from God to every individual.

The final step in the progress of this discovery was when I looked into the meaning of the original Hebrew language of this verse. The Hebrew word translated as *get* and *produce* is the word *asah* (pronounced ah-SAH). This word has a variety of meanings and among them are: to *make, earn, bring into being, or to create.* What a concept! **Humans can create wealth**. Wealth that did not formerly exist in a manifested form can come into being whenever humans *will* and *work* to bring it about. This study established my understanding so firmly that I now declare this everywhere I go and to everyone who will listen. (In the OT, *asah* is used both of God and humans creating and making.)

When human beings realize this truth and allow it to work in their lives, things begin to change and wealth begins to flow. Nothing is more empowering in your economic life than to know that you don't have to steal wealth, you don't have to cheat for wealth, you don't even have to hope for luck (gamble) to get wealth—you can create wealth because you have the ability. Ability means God supplies the mind, means, and motivation to create wealth.

Mind: the capacity, ideas, and wisdom to create wealth
Means: the methods, processes, and the opportunities to create wealth
Motivation: the empowerment, strength, and the persistence to create wealth

The ability to produce wealth does come from God, for without these God-given endowments, it would be impossible for humans to produce wealth. When God declared this to Israel after their emancipation from slavery, He was confirming—making good on His covenant—with Abraham, Isaac, and Jacob.

Actually, this upholding of the *wealth covenant* (or the prosperity aspect of the covenant) has its foundation with Adam in Genesis. God reminds His people in Isaiah 54:10 (NLT), "*For the mountains may depart and the hills disappear, but even then I will remain loyal to you. My covenant of blessing will never be broken.*" The Hebrew word for *blessing* in this verse is *shalom*. Shalom is commonly understood as simply meaning "peace," but it is much richer than merely that one word. Shalom also means *health, welfare,* or *prosperity*. It presents peace as a sound, whole, and prosperous state physically, materially, emotionally, and spiritually.

The God of the Wealth Covenant has a fantastic promise for your shalom. The prophet Jeremiah has given us the voice of the LORD in revealing this promise. Jeremiah 29:11 says, "For I know the plans I have for you," declares the LORD, "plans to prosper [shalom] you and not to harm you, plans to give you hope and a future."

He calls this promise, a plan. [Hebrew = intention, a devised plan, or a planned purpose. Or it can be said to refer to God's wonderful, breathtaking, awe-inspiring thoughts and purposes about you and for you.] The verb form of this word refers to devising, esteeming, or valuing something. God values you so much that he has devised a peace and prosperity plan. So, believe it, receive it, and live it!

This is a covenant of blessing, prosperity, and wealth. God's promise is not just for Israel, for He clearly states this covenant is also for the Gentiles (those who are not Jewish) who will commit themselves to Him and accept this covenant. Isaiah 56:6 (NLT) says, "*I will also bless the Gentiles who commit themselves to the LORD and serve him and love his name, who worship him and do not desecrate the Sabbath day of rest, and who have accepted his covenant.*"

You can get more detail about the wealth covenant and Deuteronomy 8:18 in a booklet entitled, "*The Wealth Covenant: The Meaning of Deuteronomy 8:18,*" available at my Web sites *KenHammonds.com* and *WealthyThinking.com*.

Because the God of Wealth created you, you have the inner wisdom, power, and possibility to produce wealth. You are somebody. You are a wealth-producing, specially designed creature called *human*. Whatever you can conceive, God will help you achieve. Any group of people or individual who has been freed from the tyranny of slavery physically and mentally, any person in the underclass, or anyone at the bottom rung of society can tap into this God-given promise. Here is another verse to spur you into action.

Lazy hands make a man poor, but diligent hands bring wealth.
$\qquad\qquad\qquad\qquad\qquad\qquad\qquad$ *Proverbs 10:4 (NIV)*

Phase Two
I: Increasing Wealth

Phase One Producing Wealth (creating/generating)
Phase Two Increasing Wealth (preserving/investing)
Phase Three Enjoying Wealth (living/celebrating)
Phase Four Sharing Wealth (caring for/empowering others)

Increasing wealth: what a nice idea. This Second Phase of the wealth cycle can be understood in two ways. First, there is the increasing of wealth, which comes from *continuing to produce* wealth. Then, there is the increasing of wealth through the *preserving and investing* of wealth.

Let's first discuss the increase of wealth by continually producing it. This idea is a valid and Scriptural concept. Many believe wealth, money, and material things should not be increased but only increased to the level of just enough to get by. But, this is not true, and certainly if one can produce wealth, it would be an underutilization of one's God-given ability and selfish not to increase the wealth to care for one's self, loved ones, and the world.

The Scriptures indicate it is natural and expected for one's financial situation to increase. I believe most of us would say we want our economic situation to increase, not decrease or stay the same. By the way, if our economic life stayed the same, it would be actually decreasing. Ever heard of inflation? So, don't be embarrassed or think you are unspiritual because you want your financial situation, your business, or your career development to increase. It's natural for the wealth in your life to increase, grow, or build. And God wants you and it to increase.

May the LORD make you increase, both you and your children.

Psalm 115:14 (NIV)

The NIV Study Bible has the footnote at the phrase, "make you increase." It says this phrase refers to increasing, "In numbers, wealth, and strength."

Jabez cried out to the God of Israel, "Oh, that you would bless me and enlarge my territory! Let your hand be with me, and keep me from harm so that I will be free from pain." And God granted his request.

1 Chronicles 4:10 (NIV)

Jabez – A Man with Limits

Jabez, a man born in grief, sorrow, and pain, sent up a plea to God for help. And in this plea he asks God to, "enlarge my territory." The Hebrew word for territory means a *border*. It is used of an *object marking the limit* of an area or territory. It refers to a *barrier*, or *limitation*.

Jabez was not just asking God to enlarge his land ownership and financial state, though that is a proper request. Jabez is also asking God to enlarge, or increase all the borders or limitations in his life. "Break the limits in my life." That's Jabez's prayer. "I was born in pain and self doubt and I have been limited, indeed, I've limited myself. God, please help me to take the blinders off my eyesight so I won't see my boundaries, but rather focus on the boundless potential you bring into my life."

What limits are you facing in your life? Financial, health, educational, relationships? Need expansion of your business or career? Need expansion of your surrounding environment into one that is wholesome and healthy for you and your family? Need expansion of your mind because you think too small? Do you have a *micro-mind* in a macro-world? Well, join in with the bold request Jabez placed before God. "God enlarge the limits of my life." And God answered his prayer. After all, the limits aren't God's limits; they're yours. So, do as I heard

Bishop Noel Jones preach, "Take the Limits Off God!" So now, I'll preach it to you – Take the limits off God, and watch Him enlarge every area of your life.

Caution Signs

As with all of God's blessings to us, there are warnings and caution signs with this increase in financial and material blessings.

Do not trust in extortion or take pride in stolen goods; though your riches increase, do not set your heart on them.

Psalm 62:10 (NIV)

He who oppresses the poor to increase his wealth and he who gives gifts to the rich [as bribes] both come to poverty.

Proverbs 22:16 (NIV)

Not only is it proper and right to increase one's wealth by continually producing, we can also have our money work for us. It's called investing. This is the second part of the Increasing wealth phase.

I: Increasing Wealth
God Loves Investors

After one has produced, there must be a preserving and investing of wealth if it is to increase. This is the essence of Phase Two of the wealth cycle. Increasing requires both preserving and investing that which has been produced. The work of producing wealth is of little value if the drain is greater than the income. Many have made wealth only to see it fly away as the Scriptures tell us in Proverbs 23:5 (NIV):

Cast but a glance at riches, and they are gone, for they will surely sprout wings and fly off to the sky like an eagle.

Serious thought about monetary wealth leads us to an understanding of the importance of preserving it. Much study and sound advice is necessary for the proper investment of wealth. The disciplines of saving and investing are essential for the preservation of one's hard earned wealth. Proverbs 6:6–11 (NIV) emphasizes the importance of hard work and saving wealth.

Go to the ant, you sluggard; consider its ways and be wise! It has no commander, no overseer or ruler, yet it stores its provisions in summer and gathers its food at harvest. How long will you lie there, you sluggard? When will you get up from your sleep? A little sleep, a little slumber, a little folding of the hands to rest—and poverty will come on you like a bandit and scarcity like an armed man.

If ants can instinctively understand the need to preserve their wealth (food), surely we humans can likewise understand the need to preserve our wealth. Many financial instruments are available for retaining and growing wealth, but the simplest way to preserve wealth is to avoid waste and avoid debt. Remember the words of Scripture regarding the servitude of those in debt:

The rich rules over the poor, and the borrower is the slave of the lender.
Proverbs 22:7(NRSV)

Isn't it interesting how so many people in a "free" country can so easily become enslaved by installment debt? The freedom to be a slave: what a concept!

Living Below Your Means (LBYM)

Are you living from paycheck to paycheck? Are you part of the "working broke folks"? On my Wealth Continuum, it's called Level #3: Poor (Broke). These are the broke folks making just enough to get by and to make ends meet. (See Appendix Four, *The Wealth Continuum*.) Is saving a faint dream and a dim hope for you? At the financial investment Web site *MotleyFool.com*, there was a helpful article on April 12, 2000, by Lou Ann Lofton entitled "Living Life Below Your Means."

In everyday language, LBYM means not living or spending more than your paycheck and ability to pay. It means not living off credit card and installment debt with the *illusion* of living in abundance. The quickest way to the poor house is by living beyond your paycheck and rolling up large debt. Stanley and Danko in their best selling book, *The*

Millionaire Next Door, studied American millionaires for twenty years and also state that one of the outstanding characteristics of millionaires is that they live well below their means.

Spending Your Money

Yes, spend your wealth on the things you desire, but don't squander it or live beyond what you are able. Have enough self-image and self-esteem *not* to have to keep up with the Joneses. If the truth were known, the Joneses are miserable, broke, in debt, and mentally drained from trying to keep up with themselves! Spend some of your wealth, but don't spend all your wealth, and certainly don't spend *more* than your wealth. Proper spending, yes, but avoiding lust and avarice is also part of this Second Phase of the Divine Wealth Cycle. The discipline of proper spending will greatly assist you in wealth building and preservation.

Many who believe they are financially well off are not. They live off 95 to 98 percent of their income. Some who are in debt live off 100 percent or more of their incomes. Even living off 80 percent of your income is probably not adequate for enjoying wealth. To be *really* living is to live on 20 to 10 percent of your wealth. Well, maybe not now, but it's something we all can work toward if we are interested in extraordinary financial freedom and abundance. My personal short-term goal is to live off 60 percent.

Warning! Be diligent and never let up on preserving your wealth for one moment. There's always someone out there who wants to snatch your hard earned money. Don't give it up. Have a spending plan for your money, and stick to it. One moment of weakness can ruin your life. Your money sometimes just "disappears."

You earn wages, only to put them in a purse with holes in it. This is what the LORD Almighty says: "Give careful thought to your ways."
Haggai 1:6–7 (NIV)

Your wages disappear as though you were putting them in pockets filled with holes! This is what the LORD Almighty says: "Consider how things are going for you!"
Haggai 1:6–7 (NLT)

The Bible clearly speaks of the trans-cultural phenomenon of disappearing money. The Bible's illustration is that of putting your money into a bag, purse, or pocket "with holes in it." (And haven't we all been there?) Watching your dollars fall through your pockets or purse is not the symbol you want for *your* hard-earned money. The prophet Haggai, a financial counselor in charge of getting the Jews to give money for the rebuilding of the temple in Jerusalem, says, "Consider your ways" That is to say, "Think about how things are going for you!"

Think about your lifestyle and your spending. The keys for keeping your moneybag patched up, full, and running over are obedience, intelligence, and diligence to God's principles of wealth. Also, be determined to think about how you are living, and radically remove any self-destructive financial behavior from your lifestyle. Remember, God wants you to be wealthy, but having a "holey" purse will not help you get there.

A Quotable Quote

It ain't a sin being broke, but it is mighty inconvenient.
—**African American Church Saying**

Phase Three
E: Enjoying Wealth
The Joy of Livin' F.A.T

The Third Phase of the wealth cycle helps combat the addiction to work (workaholism). Phase Three says, "Don't just produce and increase wealth, but take time to enjoy the wealth by really living and celebrating life."

This is the joy of Livin' F.A.T—Full, Abundant, and True to God. The Scriptures often speak of living F.A.T.

Phase One **Producing Wealth** (creating/generating)
Phase Two **Increasing Wealth** (preserving/investing)
Phase Three **Enjoying Wealth** (living/celebrating)
Phase Four **Sharing Wealth** (caring for/empowering others)

He that is of a proud heart stirreth up strife: but he that putteth his trust in the LORD shall be made fat.

Proverbs 28:25 (KJV)

They shall still bring forth fruit in old age; they shall be fat and flourishing.

Psalm 92:14 (KJV)

Enjoy Wealth, Success, and Life from God

Humans were originally created to enjoy God, self, and others. Yes, with all of our big problems, we humans can still enjoy success on this planet. The philosopher of the Book of Ecclesiastes eloquently speaks concerning this phase of the wealth cycle.

Enjoy life with your wife, whom you love.

Ecclesiastes 9:9 (NIV)

However many years a man may live, let him enjoy them all.

Ecclesiastes 11:8 (NIV)

Moreover, when God gives any man wealth and possessions, and enables him to enjoy them, to accept his lot and be happy in his work—this is a gift of God.

Ecclesiastes 5:19 (NIV)

Enjoying God, enjoying work, enjoying one's life, family, and friends— now that's part of the *normal* Christian life.

Work—yes, *hard* work—is endorsed by the Scriptures. Workaholism, however, is not. Working for the sake of work alone and avoiding the development of the other areas of one's life cannot be peddled off as God's work ethic. This addiction places family, spiritual development, health, and life in jeopardy for the sake of "the job." Are you a workaholic? If you are, then it's time to get your life back in perspective. Stop and smell the roses. Enjoy your family, preserve your health, and worship your God.

Phase Four
S: Sharing Wealth
Empowerment, Not Robbery

We now arrive at the Fourth Phase of God's Wealth Cycle—Sharing Wealth. Sharing wealth has the twofold responsibility of caring for the weak and empowering others. This is a powerful principle of wealth allocation and renewal within any system—social, economic, or otherwise. In order for wealth to benefit all the people of a system, the created wealth must be shared.

| **Phase One**
Producing Wealth
(creating/generating) |
| **Phase Two**
Increasing Wealth
(preserving/investing) |
| **Phase Three**
Enjoying Wealth
(living/celebrating) |
| **Phase Four**
Sharing Wealth
(caring for/empowering others) |

Command them to do good, to be rich in good deeds, and to be generous and willing to share.

1 Timothy 6:18 (NIV)

Caring for the Weak

Sharing wealth encourages those possessing wealth to give to others. The moral strength of any human system is its ability to take care of the members of the group who are unable to care for themselves. It is the system's obligation to care for the weak. Many members of a societal group may be unable to produce as much as others. Some may be unable to economically produce at all. But yet, through the benevolence of the group, they are all valued and cared for.

Empowering Others

Sharing wealth also means empowering those who are able. Only those who are willing to receive and act will realize the value of being empowered. Then, the empowered person will be able to move to Phase One and personally produce wealth through ingenuity, innovation, and diligent labor. These empowered ones will be able to provide for themselves and be productive members of society. The wealth cycle continues. Now, they will also flow with the cycle by Producing, Increasing, Enjoying, and then Sharing their wealth with others.

This generosity phase of the wealth cycle is not a contribution without purpose or direction. Neither is it a wasteful handout. It's a "hand up," the gift of empowering others to do that which they are without aid unable to do. Furthermore, it is a wise thing to do because everyone benefits from the sharing of wealth in this manner. Withholding wealth distribution means wealth for the few and poverty for the many. However, the twofold sharing of wealth in the P.I.E.S. wealth cycle means enough wealth for everyone.

The Wealth Cycle Must be a Cycle

When I began developing the P.I.E.S. wealth cycle, I originally ended with E: Enjoying Wealth. But, I thank God for revealing to me the last important stage of the cycle. For, if the cycle ends with only hedonistic enjoyment for a few, then that system is not a blessing but a curse to humanity. Any person wrapped up in himself or herself is a mighty small package. If the cycle ends with enjoyment, it is not a cycle at all, but rather a *dead end.*

Most Bible students know of the condition of the Dead Sea (also known as the Salt Sea) in Palestine. The sea is fed primarily by the Jordan River to the north. But, at its southern end, there is no major outlet. The Dead Sea receives but never fully gives. As a result, the sea has a large salt concentration. No marine life can exist and its water is unfit for drinking. So, instead of being a living, vital body of water providing life and growth to other life forms, this Dead Sea is *dead.* The forty-eight–mile long, eleven–mile wide sea is a lifeless, comatose natural phenomenon that serves no useful purpose. It only serves as an example of what we as humans should not be.

No individual or system can afford to only take and receive. If it does, it will be doomed to failure because it does not supply help and nourishment to others. Sooner or later, it will not even find enough sources for its own survival. Its mode of existing by *always taking* will be the cause of its own demise.

Thus, to offer complete enjoyment of wealth by all, the P.I.E.S. cycle must in fact be a cycle. Will you exist as a Dead Sea, or will you develop into a thriving source of life for all who come into your presence? Will your prosperity dry up because it is not released, or will your life be saturated with blessing because your prosperity has been shared as a source of benefit to others? Creating wealth should enrich everyone. Any individual or system seeking to be living, thriving, and profiting will also include sharing as a key element.

A P.I.E.S. adaptation of a Benjamin Disraeli quotation will fit well here. He said, "The greatest good we can do for others is not to [merely] share our riches, but to assist [them] in revealing their own."

Historical Note: Benjamin Disraeli was prime minister of England first in 1868 and again from 1874 to 1880. He was a Jewish-Christian and was known for his public outcry of the failure of the church and state to fulfill their obligations to improve the working and living conditions of common people. When he was in office, he changed the laws to improve housing and working conditions.

The twelfth-century philosopher Moses Maimonides (pronounced mi-MON-neh-deez) believed the highest level of personal assistance was enabling another person to become self-sufficient through a gift or loan, or helping a person to develop a skill or obtain employment.

And we urge you, brothers, warn those who are idle, encourage the timid, help the weak, be patient with everyone.

1 Thessalonians 5:14 (NIV)

We must both *empower* the able and *care for* the weak. These are the two sides of the sharing coin. The apostle Paul reminds us we must warn, encourage, help, or be patient with people as is appropriate for the situation.

George Gilder presents the concern and challenge of prosperity in an article entitled "Prophets of Boom," in *Wired* magazine (September 1999). Gilder, an authority in technology, economics, and entrepreneurial wealth creation, reveals his concern in an economic boom. He says, "I worry that so many people don't have any comprehension of how to create wealth by serving others." He also states the challenge, or the downside, to economic prosperity is that it can easily be subverted by an "outbreak in hedonism" (living one's life for pleasure alone). I believe prosperity without hedonism is possible, but it requires strong personal values and a genuine concern for others.

God Wants You to be Wealthy: A P.I.E.S. View

The P.I.E.S. perspective of wealth building also further defines the wealth declaration. The P.I.E.S. wealth cycle meaning for the declaration, "God wants you to be wealthy" is: "God wants you to produce, increase, enjoy, and share wealth."

Tithing: A Wealth-building Strategy?

The Old Testament

A significant guide for giving started in the OT thousands of years ago. It's called *tithing* (giving one tenth). Abraham, the Father of the Faith (around 2100 BC), is the biblical prototype for this kind of giving. He freely gave a special tithe of his combat wealth to an OT king/priest named Melchizedek for the successful search and rescue mission of his nephew, Lot (Genesis 14:11–24). It was Abraham's display of thanks to God for his victory. He is the first tither mentioned in the Bible and thus, the Father of Tithing (giving wealth to God). This tithe is defined as: freely giving one tenth of one's wealth to God or His work.

Under the Law of Moses (1400 BC), the tithe was extended to a regular ritualistic, yet practical, giving of money, fruit, grain, oil, the juice from grapes, and livestock by the people of Israel for the support of the priesthood and for the support of the poor. Moses calls the tithe holy (Hebrew: *qodesh*—consecrated, dedicated, a sacred thing, set apart as a special gift) to the LORD God. [LORD, all capital letters, = God's Name, *Jehovah* or more correctly, *Yahweh*.]

The New Testament

In the NT, Jesus commended the scribes and Pharisees for their faithfulness in tithing. (This was one of few times, and maybe the only time, he praised them for anything!) Paul never used the word tithe in his writings but is careful not to explicitly reject the powerful, time-honored tithing custom. Though he radically reshapes the Christian reinterpretation of the OT law, he is careful not to dismiss the tithing spirit of giving.

Apostle Paul Speaks of Bountiful Giving

At times, Paul seems to exceed the tenth when he uses phrases like, "sowing [giving] bountifully" in 2 Corinthians 9:6. Some expositors say Paul is referring to the tithe here, but that is unlikely. As an ex-Pharisee, Paul certainly knows how to use the word tithe when he wants to refer to it. The Greek word used here, *eulogia* [pronounced you-low-GEE-ah, with a hard "g," as in "get."], is translated, *bountifully or generously,* and refers to a consecrated gift which is freely and spontaneously bestowed and that which springs from unconditional love.

This was probably *beyond* a tenth, for Paul was amazed at how the congregation in Corinth gave out of their extreme poverty. Because of this bountiful giving, Paul assures them that God's outpour of abundant blessings will certainly come upon them.

The Tenth in the Non-Religious World

This tithing (tenth) model is also the practice of many wealthy individuals and non-religious people. Motivational author Dr. Joseph Murray calls it, "The Magic Law of Tithing." Millionaires and millionaire trainers Robert Allen and Mark Victor Hansen hardily encourage giving the tenth in their millionaire curriculum called *The Enlightened Millionaire Program.* This wealth-building program grooms people concerning how to become enlightened, sharing millionaires. As a matter of fact, Allen and Hansen call tithing and prayer two powerful alternative wealth strategies.

A Universal Sharing Principle

It seems as if this tithing strategy is a universal human sharing principle recorded as early as the time of Abraham. Thus, there's a 4,000-year history of this bountiful sharing of wealth. That's far enough back in human history to really mean something!

Indeed, when you use this tithing wealth strategy and other wealth-building principles of Scripture, you will become a powerful patron, spreading the wealth of God's blessings to others. And, amazingly, these abundant blessings will return right back to you, the giver!

A Flood of Blessings

Malachi (around 400 BC) describes the results of this wealth strategy in dramatic fashion:

"Bring the whole tithe into the storehouse, that there may be food in my house. Test me in this," says the LORD Almighty, "and see if I will not throw open the floodgates of heaven and pour out so much blessing that you will not have room enough for it."

Malachi 3:10 (NIV)

God's Wealth Cycle is a comprehensive system, providing for the financial and material needs of the individual and society. If this liberating cycle is pursued, it brings economic prosperity to all. However, if it is ignored, the resulting economic inequities lead to much poverty and pain.

CHAPTER 6

The Best Creating Wealth Seminar Ever!

In this chapter, we will discuss:

✦ The Money Parable
✦ Some "how to" Lessons for Entrepreneurs
✦ P.I.E.S. Interpretation of the Money Parable
✦ Twenty-one Secrets for Producing More Money

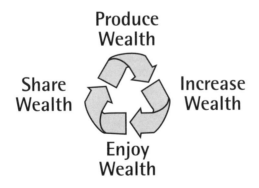

Jesus' Financial Seminar on How to Produce More Money

The Parable of Money

*J*esus taught a great deal about money. He instructed business-
men, housewives, and the common laborer. Jesus taught seven
obligations we have with money.

Seven Obligations with Money

1. Produce it.
2. Value it.
3. Place it in proper perspective.
   (It is important, but it's after God, spiritual things, people, relationships, and the other really important things in life like physical
   and mental health. Enjoy life even if you don't have all the money
   you desire. Enjoy God, people, and yourself.)
4. Give it to God. (For activities that advance the worship, work, and
   Word of God.)
5. Invest it wisely.
6. Share it with others.
7. Pay taxes on it.

So, as you can see from the list above, Jesus taught God's Wealth
Cycle—P.I.E.S. (Producing, Increasing, Enjoying, Sharing wealth) Jesus

powerfully illustrates the P.I.E.S. cycle in one of his most famous stories. In Matthew chapter twenty-five Jesus told not only an interesting story, but gave the best creating wealth seminar ever!

The story is about a rich businessman who was about to go on a trip for an extended period of time. The man called his three chief servants together and gave them each some money (talents) to manage and multiply (assume active stewardship) while he was away. One denomination of money during NT times was the talent. A talent today would be equivalent to about $500,000.00. (See the sidebar at the end of the chapter if you want more details.)

So, in Jesus' Money Parable, he gave one entrepreneurial servant five talents (2.5 million dollars) another two talents (1 million dollars), and the last servant one talent ($500,000). He gave each one what he could handle. When the master returned, both Mr. Five Talents and Mr. Two Talents had doubled their money (5 million and 2 million dollars, respectively). What a great performance! However, Mr. One Talent had done nothing except bury his **money** in the ground.

This story is commonly called "The Parable, or Story, of the Talents." Unfortunately, most people misunderstand the story. They think it is primarily about using your personal talents or gifts. That is a proper application of the secondary level of this story. However, the story is primarily a story about money—how to manage it, make it, and multiply it.

Of course, in its wider context, this money story vividly illustrates the obligation before us to carefully utilize our possessions and to aggressively move up to full productivity and wealth in our lives. Jesus uses this money theme as the catalyst for applying the message of productivity to every area of our lives.

So, I'd like to correct the misinterpretation of the traditional title and give it its true economic interpretation. It is best entitled something like: "The Parable about Managing, Making, and Multiplying Money", but in keeping with the theme of other titles given to Jesus' discourses, I'll call it "The Parable of the Dependable and Lazy Money Managers." It is the greatest and most well known of Jesus' financial seminars and to give it a modern advertisement flair: it is the best creating wealth seminar ever! In this story, Jesus gives us a wonderful foundation for making money and building wealth. So, if money has thus far eluded you and you're saying, "Show me the money!", Jesus' Money Parable will give you the power to see it.

The Three Parables of Matthew 24–25: Primary Human Relationships

"The Parable of the Dependable and Lazy Money Managers" is part of the last group of Jesus' three teaching stories in Matthew. These three stories illustrate how to live abundantly in God's kingdom. They show the correct thinking and proper actions for kingdom people. The three stories are about relationships.

Matthew Chapters 24–25 are known as the Olivet Discourse. The day before his arrest and trial, Jesus gives this last teaching to his followers about life as citizens of God's kingdom. He gave this discourse on the Mount of Olives, which is east, just outside Jerusalem; hence the title, Olivet Discourse. This prophetic and practical speech includes three parables. Each parable vividly illustrates how God's people are to live until Jesus returns.

The first two parables are "The Parable of the Dependable and Evil Household Managers" (24:45–51) and "The Parable of the Wise and Foolish Virgins" (25:1–13).

In "The Parable of the Dependable and Evil Household Managers" (focused on properly managing your people), Jesus illustrates for us the necessity of a believer's relationship to people and the proper treatment of people by a manager or believer. Today, we commonly call this the horizontal relationship, referring to the importance of good, wholesome, and loving relationships to people. The Church has always stressed the importance of "treating our neighbors right."

"The Parable of the Wise and Foolish Virgins" (focused on properly managing your spiritual life), illustrates the necessity of a right relationship to God through His Son. Today, we commonly call this the vertical relationship, referring to the importance of our spiritual relationship to the Father.

Summary:
Virgins Parable: managing your spiritual life
Household Managers Parable: managing your people

The two relationships of these two parables:
Relationship # 1: our vertical relationship to God (R1) (Matthew 25:1–13)
Relationship #2: our horizontal relationship to people (R2) (Matthew 24:45–51)

Correctly, the Church has emphasized the necessity of this two-relationships model of human interaction: the vertical (up to God) and the horizontal (out to fellow humans). These relationships are commonly diagrammed as shown below.

The Two-Relationships Model (God & People)

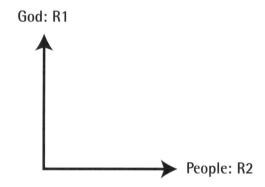

This diagram is a valuable visual tool for helping to illustrate these two relationships. However, this two-relationships diagram is limited because it does not take into account an important third relationship of life described in the third parable, "The Parable of the Dependable and Lazy Money Managers" (focused on properly managing your money).

Jesus' third parable is about a right relationship to our possessions and productivity. It is about what we produce with our God-given resources. Our relationship to money and things is a valid part of our overall spiritual development. God is concerned about every aspect of our lives. This parable illustrates the importance of utilizing our resources (knowledge, skills, material things, and time) to become fully functioning subjects of God's kingdom.

Summary:
Virgins Parable: managing your spiritual life
Household Managers Parable: managing your people
Money Managers Parable: managing your money

The three relationships of these three parables:
- ✦ Relationship # 1: our relationship to God (R1)
- ✦ Relationship # 2: our relationship to people (R2)
- ✦ Relationship # 3: our relationship to our possessions (money, material things, and inner resources) and our productivity (our professional, occupational, and volunteer life) (R3)

You can more easily remember the three relationships this way:

Our God, Our Neighbor, and Our Possessions

So, God empowers us in three primary human relationships, which can be diagrammed as follows:

The Three-Relationships Model
(God, People, and Possessions)

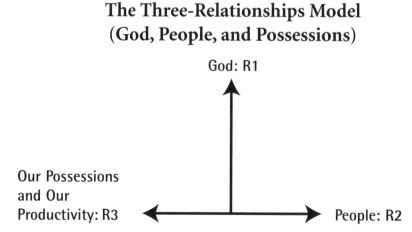

God: R1

Our Possessions and Our Productivity: R3

People: R2

The three relationships model better explains the balance God wants us to have in our Christian lives, and the diagram can become a great teaching tool, with which everyone can identify. Observe the center arrow pointing to God as the center point and balancing location for the other two relationships. This chart is not meant to show which relationship is the most important, but rather, that all three are important.

Some may believe that the spiritual person only needs a right relationship to God and that people are of secondary importance. Surely, God is first. However, your relationship to God is not less important than your relationship to people. The Scriptures make it clear that if your relationship with God is right, then your relationship with people will also be right.

Those who say, "I love God," and hate their brothers or sisters, are liars; for those who do not love a brother or sister whom they have seen, cannot love God whom they have not seen.

1 John 4:20 (NRSV)

I am also adding, based upon "The Parable of the Dependable and Lazy Money Managers," the idea that if your relationship with God is right, your relationship with money and your possessions will also be right. The question for believers is, "Is our relationship to money and material things as pure, good, honest, spiritual, and productive as our relationship with God?" I believe it should be.

 A KH Quotable Quote

*Is your relationship to money and material things
as pure, good, honest, spiritual, and productive
as your relationship with God?*

The Church has emphasized the importance of serving and worshipping God. Also, it makes great attempts to help people deal with each other. However, the Church has not adequately dealt with how a believer should relate to his or her money, resources, possessions, and personal productivity. God is also concerned about us producing our money, building our wealth, and using our resources for financing the kingdom of God, the betterment of mankind, and our own personal enjoyment.

With this background, we are ready to read the entire story and apply the P.I.E.S. interpretation.

The Parable of the Talents
Matthew 25:14–30, NIV

(14)"Again, it will be like a man going on a journey, who called his servants and entrusted his property to them. (15) To one he gave five talents of money, to another two talents, and to another one talent, each according to his ability. Then he went on his journey. (16) The man who had received the five talents went at once and put his money to work and gained five more. (17) So also, the one with the two talents gained two more.(18) But the man who had received the one talent went off, dug a hole in the ground and hid his master's money."

(19)"After a long time the master of those servants returned and settled accounts with them.(20) The man who had received the five talents brought the other five. 'Master,' he said, 'you entrusted me with five talents. See, I have gained five more.' (21) His master replied, 'Well done, good and faithful servant! You have been faithful with a few things; I will put you in charge of many things. Come and share your master's happiness!' (22) The man with the two talents also came. 'Master,' he said, 'you entrusted me with two talents; see, I have gained two more.'(23) His master replied, 'Well done, good and faithful servant! You have been faithful with a few things; I will put you in charge of many things. Come and share your master's happiness!'"

(24) "Then the man who had received the one talent came. 'Master,' he said, 'I knew that you are a hard man, harvesting where you have not sown and gathering where you have not scattered seed. (25) So I was afraid and went out and hid your talent in the ground. See, here is what belongs to you.'"

(26) "His master replied, 'You wicked, lazy servant! So you knew that I harvest where I have not sown and gather where I have not scattered seed? (27) Well then, you should have put my money on deposit with the bankers, so that when I returned I would have received it back with interest. (28) Take the talent from him and give it to the one who has the ten talents.'"

(29) "For everyone who has will be given more, and he will have an abundance. Whoever does not have, even what he has will be taken from him. (30) And throw that worthless servant outside, into the darkness, where there will be weeping and gnashing of teeth."'

A P.I.E.S. Interpretation of the Parable

This interpretation assumes you have read Chapter 5 of this book, *God's Wealth Cycle: P.I.E.S.* (Remember from Chapter 5, P.I.E.S. stands for Producing Wealth, Increasing Wealth, Enjoying Wealth, and Sharing Wealth. This is the wealth cycle, God's Wealth Cycle.) Notice that the acronym P.I.E.S. in the context of this story is out of the regular P-I-E-S order. Our story starts with the Sharing wealth phase.

First: Sharing Wealth (S) (verses 14–15)

The master had already Produced, Increased, and Enjoyed his wealth. He now empowers the servants and uses wisdom by distributing to each servant according to his ability to produce.

At the social-systems level, this is at the heart of extending wealth throughout all levels of a society. Empowering others must be a part of any system if it is to properly grow and survive. It doesn't matter if it is a family, a marriage, a football team, a basketball team, a work group, a church, a state, or a country. People must first be empowered before they can produce real, positive wealth for the system.

Second: Producing and Increasing Wealth (P and I)
(verses 16–23a) [a = first sentence of the verse]

At the personal level, the first element in spreading wealth is producing wealth. Individuals must use their creative energies to develop wealth that flows from within. Only then will they possess wealth enough to distribute and share with others.

The five-and two-talent men are empowered. They immediately launched their business enterprises. They put this money to work (managed, made, multiplied). Can you imagine the talking, studying, praying, and working they had to do to double their monies? They produced (P) and increased (I) their wealth. This is described in the text as, gained more. They greatly increased their level of wealth through investments and business savvy. The master replied to each of them, "Excellent job, you valuable and reliable servant!"

God requires (demands) that each individual produce at the highest level of his or her personal ability. He has given each of us the ability to produce. No, we all don't have the same level of ability, but we do have *some* God-given ability to produce and serve. Other Scriptures also make it clear that we all have at least one gift from God, given to us for the common good and benefit of the whole Body of Christ. As 1 Corinthians 12:7 (NIV) says, "Now to each one the manifestation of the Spirit [your gift] is given for the common good."

The apostle Paul also declares that each of us "has his own gift from God; one has this gift, another has that [gift]" (1 Corinthians 7:7, NIV). Because God has endowed us with gifts, we have no excuse for being barren and uncreative (buried and hidden in a hole in the ground). This is the heart of this parable.

In another passage, Jesus insists on spiritual and material productivity from each believer and declares that we bring glory to the Father when we, "bear much fruit, showing yourselves to be my disciples" (John 15:8, NIV). Again, in John 15:16 (NIV), Jesus declares a startling truth, "You did not choose me, but I chose you and appointed you to go and bear fruit—fruit that will last. Then the Father will give you whatever you ask in my name."

Certainly, personal productivity is a requirement of spiritual life; yet, it is much more than merely a required drudgery. It is a high and lofty privilege to serve the God of the universe and to be empowered by Him to serve humanity. God loves humans so much He has gifted them to support and serve one another in love. That is how humans show love to each other. It is not in lip service only, but in the sharing of self through the actions of service. The apostle John says it best in his little epistle (1 John 3:18, NRSV), "Little children, let us love, not in word or speech, but in truth and action."

Can the Lord say to you regarding your work and your productivity, "Excellent job, you valuable and reliable servant"?

Third: Enjoying Wealth (verse 23c)
[c = third sentence of the verse]

Now, because of their hard work, the master commends the two reliable and profitable servants and gives them greater responsibilities. He tells them to, "Come and share your master's happiness," or as the NKJV reads, "Enter into the joy of your lord." Yes, they now get to enjoy the wealth and the recognition that comes with a job well done.

On the other hand, the response of Mr. One Talent is pitiful. He responded, first of all, by describing his master as "a hard man." (Greek: *sklēpos = harsh, strict, stubborn,* or *cruel.*) This boss was a tough, no-nonsense kind of guy.

The servant describes this master wealth builder as one "who is harvesting where you have not sown and gathering where you have not scattered seed." This phrase identifies the master as having a reputation for being an outstanding entrepreneur and creator of wealth.

Furthermore, we can assume this master wealth builder taught his young budding entrepreneurs the lessons of the game of business, the tricks of the trade. He perhaps taught them some of the principles of the MBA Entrepreneurship Program at Harvard Business School (HBS), like Course #1610, *Building Businesses in Turbulent Times* (an actual class at HBS focusing on identifying and securing business resources, managing challenges and risks, and developing a network for building a successful business as an independent entrepreneur).

His, however, would be an Independent Study Course #1010, entitled *Developing Wealth-Building Strategies and Organizational Systems for Doubling Your Money.* (By the way, doubling one's money was a common occurrence during first-century business dealings. During this era, ordinary investors would receive high interest rates on their money. The bankers (KJV: the exchangers) would pay investors 12 percent on their money.)

This home study course would have perhaps been based on his unpublished book manuscript entitled *Ten Powerful Entrepreneurial Lessons for Emerging Businesses: How to Make 100 percent on Your Money.* The master wealth builder's Ten Lessons are listed below.

Ten Powerful Entrepreneurial Lessons for Emerging Businesses

This great entrepreneur and business coach taught them how to:

1. Organize for business success.
2. Set and achieve massive business goals.
3. Take calculated risks.
4. Build a business network.
5. Recognize and seize business opportunities.
6. Recognize value.
7. Perform effective negotiation techniques.
8. Sell a product.
9. Serve customers and suppliers.
10. Invest for the short term and long term.

Evidently, this entrepreneur trainer was a good teacher if two of his students could double their money. He was impressed with the performance of the two productive servants. However, the master was extremely harsh with the unproductive servant. He called him by some not so flattering names. (I would not recommend this response today as a way for making friends.) He described the servant as, "You wicked, lazy servant." This servant had a no-care attitude. Don't you get upset when you have loaned a person something of great value to you, but his or her response is a no-care attitude? Those with a no-care attitude treat the precious and valuable with carelessness and disrespect.

No Joy for a Lazy Person

It is sad, but true: a lazy person will not enjoy wealth. The lazy servant in our story wasted the master's wealth. Therefore, he was thrown outside the pleasures of the master's house and the cycle of wealth. He was thrown out into the cycle of poverty, where there is economic obscurity and gloom (darkness). (verse thirty, "throw that worthless servant outside.") This harsh economic condition (poverty) would cause him great spiritual, social, and emotional stress. Outside the estate, there was weeping and chattering of teeth. The word gnashing refers to a chattering of teeth together because of cold.

I know some are convinced that the master threw this man into *hell* because he misused the master's money. But that doesn't seem to be the case in the original language and the true economic interpretation of this context. This man was simply and rightly put out of the master's house. He now had to make it on his own. He is out in the cold. Of course, this is tough punishment for a lazy man. Before this "sentencing," he had it made in the shade in his master's fine estate. Just imagine being put out into world with no money, no job, a no-care attitude, and a lazy spirit!

The Rich Get Richer

Want to know why the rich keep getting richer? The master's statement in verses twenty-eight and twenty-nine tells us the powerful secret, "Take the talent from him and give it to the one who has the ten talents. For everyone who has will be given more, and he will have an abundance. Whoever does not have, even what he has will be taken from him."

Does this seem unfair to you? And without the P.I.E.S. economic interpretation, it may seem so. But, understanding the master's statement above in an economic sense means that those who have produced wealth *continue to receive it* even after they have stopped active engagement in production. How? Consider the two examples below:

1. They will continue to receive wealth through interest, residual checks, additional profits, stock increases, rents being paid to them, bonuses, royalties, etc.
2. They are rewarded for their excellent work in ways they aren't expecting. They don't need to pursue money because money comes to them! Have you ever known or heard of someone like that? Why is it that money just seems to come to some people, but it avoids others? These "money magnets" have the right attitude and the right systems for attracting money. It's just the P.I.E.S wealth cycle in action.

It's not so much the master who is personally being harsh, it's more the harsh economic realities of anyone not adhering to God's Wealth Cycle.

And this "taking from" the lazy servant and his subsequently being "thrown out into poverty" is the right judgment. These are the expected consequences of his actions (or *lack* of action).

When the servant described his master as, "harsh, merciless, and cruel," he was thinking about what the master was going to do to him, and that outside the wealthy estate of his master was a harsh, merciless, cruel world. For a lazy man or woman or a wealth destroyer, the world is a pretty cold place. Outside the warm home of productive living there is the cold life of a lazy, careless, unproductive, and destructive existence which results in chattering teeth and economic gloom. Ignoring God's Wealth Cycle is an invitation to economic suicide.

The attitude and actions of this lazy servant caution us that sometimes when wealth is shared, it is not appreciated as an empowerment. The recipient must act with diligence to receive the benefit.

Economic gloom (poverty) is inevitable if one is not following the P.I.E.S. cycle. This will be the experience of any family, society, or country that ignores God's Universal Wealth Cycle. I trust you will apply P.I.E.S. to your own personal economic development and the building of wealth in your life.

A Summary of Jesus' Financial Seminar
Twenty-one Secrets for Producing More Money

So much is in this parable. From this story, we can glean many secrets (principles, actions, or ideas not often utilized effectively) for making money, building wealth, and becoming abundantly productive in our lives. The actions and attitudes of Mr. Two Talents and Mr. Five Talents are important examples for us to follow.

Most of these twenty-one secrets are rooted in the same foundation as the single mother of 2 Kings Chapter 4. They utilized their EKG'S (experience, knowledge, gifts, and skills). If you utilize your EKG'S to the best of your ability, you will be abundantly productive. The twenty-one secrets are listed below.

1. Be a self-starter.

2. Approach wealth building with the right attitude.

3. Work hard and work intelligently.

4. Learn the business skills of selling, trading, buying, and negotiation. They are essential to producing wealth.

5. Using whatever God gives you will bring success.

6. God can give you the ability to make 100 percent profit on your money. (Also, Jesus affirms that honorable profit making is good.)

7. God dislikes laziness. He is displeased with those who "bury" their God-given resources and thereby become barren.

8. Courage is important in business success and in doing God's will.

9. Diligence in work and persistence are important in business success.

10. Fear will keep you from realizing God's best for your life.

11. Don't compare yourself with anyone else. It doesn't matter what God gives them; just work with what God gives you.

12. Economic disaster awaits those who do not follow God's will and God's way.

13. A no-care attitude about money will lead to poverty.

14. God has already empowered us to do great things. He's given us the goods.

15. We should immediately get busy doing God's work. (The immediate task could be preparing yourself now spiritually, educationally, physically, financially, etc. for your spiritual, occupational, and financial future.)

16. We can greatly increase our level of wealth through investments and business savvy.

17. God requires (demands) that each individual produce at the highest level of his or her personal ability.

18. Being financially responsible will lead to the enjoyment of wealth and safety, but fiscal irresponsibility will lead to economic disaster.

19. The best money managers and wealth producers have mentors.

20. If you have wealth, share your knowledge and resources with others and train them in the Ten "how to" Lessons of the business game.

21. Finally, don't sit around idly waiting for Jesus to return. Go out, get busy, do business, and build wealth until he comes. In another financial seminar story, Jesus says this:

And he called his ten servants, and delivered them ten pounds, and said unto them, 'Occupy till I come'. But his citizens hated him, and sent a message after him, saying, 'We will not have this man to reign over us'. And it came to pass, that when he was returned, having received the kingdom, then he commanded these servants to be called unto him, to whom he had given the money, that he might know how much every man had gained by trading."

Luke 19:13–15 (KJV)

The Greek words of Jesus here indicate to *occupy* (to do business, trade, sell, buy) until he comes. The last phrase in verse fifteen, *had gained by trading,* means to make a profit by doing business. Jesus indicates here it is all right to make a profit and build wealth here on Earth while serving God in His kingdom.

Here are some other translations of the KJV phrase in verse thirteen, "occupy till I come."

NRSV: "Do business with these until I come back."
NIV: "Put this money to work," he said, "until I come back."
NLT: To invest for him while he was gone.
NKJV: "Do business till I come."

Let's stay busy with our money.

The Stewardship Message of this Story

A common application of this parable is to individual stewardship, and rightly so. This story in its immediate context is a money parable, but in its secondary, wider application, a stewardship parable. However, most Bible teachers and commentators have not recognized the twofold aspect of stewardship. Stewardship has been defined as *management over the resources of someone else, or on behalf of someone else.* As true as this statement is, stewardship is not only about the proper management of resources, it is also about productivity and creativity flowing from inner resources (wealth within you) and outer resources (wealth around you).

In our stewardship parable, the master does not reprimand his servant for managing his money (watching over it and returning it to him). He throws the servant out of the estate for not increasing his money (making more of it and returning more to him). Successful stewardship requires that we *manage* and *multiply* every resource God has made available to us.

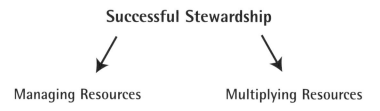

Successful Stewardship

Managing Resources   Multiplying Resources

THE MONETARY EQUIVALENT OF A BIBLICAL TALENT

The actual value of a Biblical talent has been variously interpreted by expositors as $1,000 to several thousand dollars. However, I am not so much interested in placing the exact amount of the talent, but in applying what its equivalent would be today.

I have calculated today's value of a Biblical talent as over $500,000.00. Two talent calculation descriptions are below, a simplified description and a more detailed description.

Simplified Description for My Calculation of the Value of a Talent

Each Talent is worth **23.08** years of work.
Using as a wages example, a modest annual salary of
$21,840.00 (10.50/hr) for today's laborer.

$21,840 annual salary x 23.08 years of work = **$504,000.00***
This figure, **$504,000.00**, is today's equivalent value for one talent.

* These totals are rounded off for simplicity.

Therefore:

- One talent = $500,000 (half a million dollars)
- Two talents = $1,000,000 (1 million dollars)
- Five talents = $2,500,000 (2.5 million dollars)*

* These totals are rounded off for simplicity.

A More Detailed Description for Calculating the Value of a Talent

The talent of money in NT times (Greek: talanton, pronounced TA-lan-tone) was worth 6,000 denarii (pronounced de-NA-ree-eye). A denarius was equivalent to a day's wages. Therefore, each talent was worth 23.08 years of work (6,000 denarii divided by 260 workdays per year).

If we use an average USA daily wage of $84.00 ($10.50/hour), then the annual salary would be $21,840.00. $84.00/day multiplied by 6,000 days (23 years of work) equals $504,000.00. This is the value of each talent translated into today's dollars. Thus, even one talent represents a large sum of money. This may better explain the master's reaction to the servant who was so careless as to bury this extremely valuable sum of money.

Therefore:

- One talent = $500,000 (half a million dollars)
- Two talents = $1,000,000 (1 million dollars)
- Five talents = $2,500,000 (2.5 million dollars)*

* These totals are rounded off for simplicity.

PART THREE

The Building Blocks of Wealth

 A KH Quotable Quote

*Only the building blocks set upon
a rock will have any stock.*

*And the rain descended, and the floods came, and the winds
blew, and beat upon that house; . . . yet it did not fall, because
it had its foundation on the rock.*

Matthew 7:25 (KJV, NIV)

CHAPTER 7

The First Building Block of Wealth: The Power of the Individual

In this chapter, we will discuss:

✦ The Building Blocks of Wealth
✦ The First Building Block of Wealth: The Power of the Individual
✦ Seventy-seven Powerful Attitudes of Wealth Builders

The Building Blocks of Wealth

∽ **A KH Quotable Quote** ∾

What the mind of the righteous can conceive,
God will help them achieve.

So far in Part One and Part Two, we have discussed the compatibility of spirituality and wealth and how to release the wealth builder within. We have dealt with understanding wealth, the wealth cycle, and the secrets of wealth and success. Since we now have an understanding of wealth, it is time to discuss a different perspective of wealth called the Building Blocks of Wealth. If the individual and society at large are to enjoy wealthy living, there must be the alignment of these basic building blocks of wealth. After we have started with the spiritual foundations in God, there are three basic building blocks in human society: the individual, the community, and the nation.

Together these three building blocks create a strong society and a positive environment for wealth. The individual must have the right thinking and attitude, the community must instill wealth-building habits within the individual, and the nation must promote peace and prosperity to all its residents by observing and advancing the factors that produce wealthy nations.

This chapter and the next will discuss these three building blocks and the requirements of each element. This chapter (Chapter 7) is about the attitudes that produce wealthy individuals. This is the first building block of wealth—the power of the individual. Chapter 8, Part One, is about the habits that produce wealthy communities. This is the second building block of wealth—the influence of the community. Part Two of Chapter 8 is about factors that produce wealthy nations. This is the third building block of wealth—the commitment of the nation. So, these two chapters (Chapters 7 and 8) will present the building blocks of wealth and discuss the requirements of each block for the whole of wealth development.

Shown below are the three building blocks of wealth.

✦ **The Nation (Wealthy Factors)**
✦ **The Community (Wealthy Habits)**
✦ **The Individual (Wealthy Attitudes)**

Let me speak for a moment regarding the natural order of the blocks, which flow upward from Individual (I) to Community (C), and then to the Nation (N): I-C-N. Other relationships are possible. Sometimes the order may be C-I-N, C-N-I, or N-C-I. A national, community, or individual crisis could reverse the natural order. At times, the nation leads and supports the communities to empower the individual—the N-C-I relationship. Yet, at other times the community may appeal (or demand) attention from the nation (government) to respond to the needs of the individual—the C-N-I relationship. Or, the community can shape the attitude and habits of the individual to be a force in the nation—the C-I-N relationship. A creative social dynamic occurs as the three building blocks interact, grow, and develop.

However, I feel the natural order is expressed when the individual forms the community (with interaction back and forth) and the community forms the nation.

The First Building Block of Wealth: the Power of the Individual

The first block in the graphic below is shaded because it is the subject of our first discussion.

✦ **The Nation (Wealthy Factors)**
✦ **The Community (Wealthy Habits)**
✦ **The Individual (Wealthy Attitudes)**

"As a Man Thinketh"

Thinking, attitude, mindset, outlook, belief: all of these words signify a philosophy of life by which a person functions. It determines how high (or low) a person, a family, a community, or a nation will go in life. It determines whether a person even believes he or she can go higher. I have talked with individuals in my personal coaching and development practice that actually believed God had cursed them and there was nothing better for them. They believed they were doomed to life "at the bottom." It is said, "Your attitude determines your altitude," and it's true.

Proverbs 23:7—Many Applications

- *For as a man thinketh in his heart, so is he.*
  Proverbs 23:7 (KJV)
- *For as a woman thinketh in her heart, so is she.*
  Proverbs 23:7 (women's application)
- *For as a family thinketh in its heart, so is it.*
  Proverbs 23:7 (family application)
- For as a _____ thinketh in its heart, so is _____."
  Proverbs 23:7 (application to your life: you fill in the blanks as many different times as you like.)

Other Scriptures

And there were giants in the land . . . and we were in our own sight as grasshoppers.

Numbers 13:33 (KJV)

But be ye transformed by the renewing of your mind.

Romans 12:2 (KJV)

The ingrained poverty attitude of so many people is one of the driving factors motivating me to write this wealth commentary. As I began to search the Bible to uncover and present its wealth-building principles, I made a discovery: *God wants you to be wealthy!* No, God hasn't appointed you to poverty and lack, but to wealth and full spiritual living.

Even at the cost of being misunderstood by those who believe "bottom living" is for some people, so don't try to assist them, I must declare the truth of successful and whole living as God's design for all the people of this planet. I wish to present hope. And hope starts with your thinking, your attitude.

The Wealth Builder Within

Do you know there is a wealth builder inside you? Yes, a wealth builder. Actually, I'm using "wealth builder" as a symbol of the full wealth residing within you. It is a symbol of the power of God inside you. It is a symbol of the possibilities of your lifestyle and the potential of your life's story.

It is also the "millionaire" within. The dictionary describes *million* as also meaning, *a very large or indefinitely great number.* You possess vast potential and power, and infinitely great possibilities are before you. Everyone has this millionaire inside. However, financially successful individuals and entrepreneurs have learned how to release the wealth within. The wealth is not outside you; it is in you. Indeed, literally millions of dollars in ideas, innovation, and creativity reside within you.

All the wealth *around* you cannot
be compared with the wealth *inside* you.

The wealth residing within you has been there for a long time—since your birth. Maybe you never recognized it before, but while you are reading, I hope you are becoming convinced it is there. Some of you might say, "I can't see a fully grown wealth builder. I only see the embryo of a wealth builder." But, that's okay for now, just as long as you see something! And be assured that if God has allowed you to see the wealth builder in embryo, He will bring it to full maturity as the Scripture has said: *Being confident of this, that he who began a good work in you will carry it on to completion until the day of Christ Jesus* (Philippians 1:6, NIV).

Others of you are saying, "I see the wealth builder. I see him, or I see her, and wow, does he or she look good! I see God blessing, and I see myself living according to the Word and following principles of the Word. The millionaire is large and fully grown."

✦ Moses said, "prosperity is within you"—on the tip of your tongue (your declaration). It's in your innermost being, the desire and resolve of your will (your heart). *No, the word is very near you; it is in your mouth and in your heart so you may obey it. See, I set before you today life and prosperity, death and destruction. (Deuteronomy 30:14–15, NIV)*

✦ Jesus Christ said in Luke 17:21, *The kingdom of God is within you.*

✦ Apostle John said in 1 John 4:4, *Greater is He that is within you than he that is in the world.*

✦ Apostle Paul said in 2 Timothy 1:6, *Stir up the gift of God, which is in you.*

The wealth builder inside is a free gift, a divine endowment, a spiritual gift from God.

Inside you is everything needed to accomplish what God has called you to do. (Take a moment and read that sentence again!)

Just awaken this potential, use it, and develop it. Stir up the wealth builder that is within you. Don't just "settle" anymore; be the best you can be. Apply all the great gifts and talents inside you. Remember, you are fearfully and wonderfully made!

"The wealth builder within" simply means there are possibilities. It means the residency of the Holy Spirit in you outweighs any obstacle around you. You can be debt free. You can enjoy the fat of the land. You can awaken the millionaire within. It means the Image of God and the Spirit of God in you give you million-dollar ideas.

You know this wealth builder exists by the tension within that says, "I know God has something more for me. I can feel I am so close. I just need a little push, a little encouragement, and a little more of that wealth builder mentality. I just need some strategies regarding what to do to make it. I don't know exactly where all of this is taking me, but I'll walk on by faith."

God started His million-dollar project in you long ago. You have known it for years, even though your present situation does not proclaim you to be a million-dollar person. Time and again, you've had ideas. You know they are great ideas, and they probably mean money—much money. Those great ideas come from the wealth builder within, who is talking to you. You hear it, but you just can't seem to follow through.

Perhaps you have nearly made it, or already made it to the million-dollar level or beyond. You can implement P.I.E.S even more fully in your life and teach it diligently to others. Watch their wealth improve and yours, also. Your challenge is to implement true wealth into *every area* of your life. Foster rich personal growth within, abundantly wholesome relationships with others, continued wealthy professionalism, and cherish the time you have with the people and things that really matter most to you.

The wealth builder within is extremely powerful. It can transform your present and fashion your destiny. Thank God for the wealth within, because it is more valuable than rubies and more precious than pure gold.

Critics? What Critics?

Oh, I can hear the negative thinkers and the nay sayers scoffing, "It's ridiculous to believe that everyone has a millionaire, wealth builder, or wealth inside. Some people just don't have it." Well, the difference between me as a wealthy thinker and those negative thinkers is that I believe in the great God-given wealth and possibilities in each human being. Who can say with certainty that the little infant boy thrown into the garbage heap in Africa will not grow up to be a great man and a successful and influential religious leader? I don't doubt or limit God. Do you?

By the way, this is exactly what happened to that great and extremely successful Christian leader in Nigeria, the late Archbishop Benson Idahosa (died 1998). He was a throw away garbage baby. However, God raised him up. Archbishop Idahosa was responsible for the development and growth of over 3,000 Christian churches in Nigeria and worldwide. He formed schools and was responsible for many positive educational, economic, and social changes in the country of Nigeria.

Yes, I believe in the potential within to grow and develop wildly beyond what any of us (or those negative thinkers) can think. The Scriptures clearly declare that God can do *immeasurably more than all we ask or imagine, according to his power that is at work within us* (Ephesians 3:20, NIV). I believe in the potential within because I believe God.

How to Develop a Wealth-Builder Attitude Within

Your attitude is the key to developing your wealth potential. As it is often said, "Your attitude determines your altitude." Throughout our study of wealth, we are seeking to set before you the Scriptures and the clear thinking that promote success.

For the rest of the chapter, we will survey the literature of ten books of modern success thinkers and the ancient literature of the richest man in Israel's history. Our purpose will be to discover what they have said about wisdom, work, and wealth. Wealth builders have millionaire attitudes, and we'll discover many of them in the rest of this section.

Powerful Millionaire Attitudes (PMA)

Seventy-seven Powerful Attitudes of Wealth Builders: Modeling Wealth Builders' Attitudes

This section and the next include seventy-seven of the key attitudes in framing your mindset for financial and life success. I call these positive and practical success hints, Powerful Millionaire Attitudes (PMA). This section, *Ten Books from Modern Masters* lists sixty Powerful Millionaire Attitudes, and the next section, *Powerful Millionaire Attitudes from a Well-known Billionaire,* lists seventeen Powerful Millionaire Attitudes.

Some of you may recognize PMA as Napoleon Hill's (His famous motivational book, *Think and Grow Rich*) acrostic for Positive Mental Attitude. However, in this section, PMA will also mean Powerful Millionaire Attitudes.

Powerful Millionaire Attitudes (PMA) from Ten Books of Modern Masters of Wealthy Thinking

Sixty Nuggets of Sound Advice and Attitudes from Modern Masters of Wealthy Thinking

1. *The Wealth of the World,* by John Avanzini

✆ Powerful Millionaire Attitudes ✆

- ✦ It takes faith and patience to receive wealth in your life. The first step in wealth building is sowing seeds in faith, but next must come a time of growing (patience). Finally, there is the season of harvest (reaping).
- ✦ Believe that God wants you to have wealth.
- ✦ God's wealthy Earth will produce eight primary minerals (gold, silver, copper, aluminum, iron, tin, zinc, and lead). They will generate over 21 trillion dollars in the next 20 years.
- ✦ You already have the God-given power to get wealth.

2. *The Millionaire Next Door,* by Thomas J. Stanley and William D. Danko

✆ Powerful Millionaire Attitudes ✆

The millionaire and the millionaire minded:
- ✦ Live well below their means.
- ✦ Allocate their time, energy, and money efficiently, in ways conducive to building wealth.

✦ Believe that financial independence is more important than displaying high social status.
✦ Are proficient in targeting market opportunities.
✦ Choose the right occupation.

---

3. *Acres of Diamonds,* **by Russell H. Conwell**
(Every individual should read this world-famous classic fable!)

⌒ **Powerful Millionaire Attitudes** ⌒

✦ Like Ali Hafed, the farmer in the fable, you already have acres of diamonds in your backyard. You have the wealth within. Don't die poor, sick, suffering, in rags, and disappointed that you have not found it somewhere else in the world.
✦ Everyone has within her or his reach "acres of diamonds," opportunities to get wealth right in Philadelphia. (He first gave this speech in Philadelphia, Pennsylvania. The idea, of course, is that you have opportunities for wealth right where you are.)
✦ You ought to get rich. It's your duty to get rich. If you can honestly attain riches in Philadelphia, it is your Christian and godly duty to do it.
✦ A great quote from the preacher (Conwell was a minister of the Gospel of Jesus Christ) on the need for money in the Christian's life: " . . . when we stand in the pulpit, we believe it is wicked for any man to have money—until the collection basket goes around, and then we almost swear at the people because they don't give more money. Oh, the inconsistency of such doctrines as that. Money is power, and you ought to be reasonably ambitious to have it! You ought because you can do more good with it than you can without it. Money printed your Bible, money builds your churches, money sends your missionaries, and money pays your preachers, and you would not have many of them, either, if you did not pay them."
✦ Where there is a human need, there is a great fortune.

✦ It's not *where* you are, but *who* you are, that matters.

---

4. *The Million Dollar Secret Hidden in Your Mind: The Hidden Ingredients of the Million Dollar Secret,* by Anthony Norvell

⌒ Powerful Millionaire Attitudes ⌒

Anthony Norvell's PMA from Chapter 9:
  ✦ One creative idea can make you a million dollars.
  ✦ You must build a million-dollar consciousness.
  ✦ Wealth favors the **bold**—boldness of concept and boldness of action.
  ✦ Don't pursue just money alone. Also focus on social relationships, friendships, love, inner contentment, and integrity.
  ✦ There are many ingredients to the million-dollar secret hidden in your mind. Ingredients like:
    · Give value to the world.
    · Put integrity and quality in your services and products.
    · Think of new things that will improve and change people's lives.

And he has many more throughout the rest of the book.

---

5. *Think and Grow Rich: A Black Choice,* by Dennis Kimbro and Napoleon Hill

⌒ Powerful Millionaire Attitudes ⌒

  ✦ Yes, racism and discrimination exists and will probably be constants, but never let that be an excuse for your not developing.
  ✦ Success is not a product of fate, chance, or luck; it is the result of a burning desire that knows not defeat.
  ✦ Kimbro quotes black multimillionaire A. G. Gaston, founder of Booker T. Washington Insurance Company: "I want to be rich, so I thought, 'How does a poor black man acquire wealth?'

Simple: by providing a useful service."

✦ Quoting former First Lady Eleanor Roosevelt: "No one can make you feel inferior without your consent."

✦ Quoting Marcus Garvey, twentieth century apostle of black self-empowerment and self-determination: "There is no force like success, and that is why the individual makes all efforts to surround himself throughout life with the evidence of it. …the black man must be up and doing if he will break down the prejudice of the rest of the world. We must strike out for ourselves in the course of material achievement, and by our own effort and energy present to the world those forces by which the progress of man is judged."

---

6. *Your Infinite Power to be Rich*, by Joseph Murray

∽ Powerful Millionaire Attitudes ∽

Dr. Murray's chapter titles alone speak volumes of wealth-attitude development. Below is a listing of some of the chapter titles.

Chapter 1: The Treasure House of Infinity: The infinite storehouse of ideas within you

Chapter 2: Riches are All Around You

Chapter 5: How to Pray and Grow Rich

Chapter 6: The Magic Law of Tithing

Chapter 9: All Business is God's Business

Chapter 14: Miracles of Riches through the Power of Your Words

A Wealth Affirmation: "God's wealth is circulating in my life, and there always is a Divine surplus."

A Wealth Prayer of Thanks: "God's wealth is circulating in my life. His wealth flows to me in avalanches of abundance, and I give thanks for my good now and for all of God's riches."

7. *The Instant Millionaire,* by Mark Fisher

∽ Powerful Millionaire Attitudes ∾

✦ People who wait for the "perfect conditions" never get anything done. The time for action is NOW!

✦ The magic of quantified objective: do you want to become rich? Then, write down on a piece of paper the amount of money you want and how much time you will allow yourself to acquire it.

✦ To become rich, you have to create a new self-image. Your self-image is so powerful that it unwittingly becomes your destiny.

✦ When an opportunity arises, seize it without the slightest hesitation. Don't let yourself be paralyzed by fear, which prevents so many people from living out their dreams.

✦ True wealth isn't only the acquisition of material possessions. True wealth is much broader than that. If, in searching for wealth, you lose happiness, you have lost everything. Don't let pursuing money prevent you from enjoying life.

8. *How to Think Like a Millionaire,* by Mark Fisher and Marc Allen

∽ Powerful Millionaire Attitudes ∾

✦ Quoting Helen Keller, a blind and deaf child from the age of 2 who went on to become a college graduate and a great American overcomer, thinker, and social advocate: "One can never consent to creep when one feels the impulse to soar."

✦ Most people never reach success because they give up after one or two setbacks.

✦ Success and prosperity now certainly include a balanced life.

✦ You will become as great as your dominant aspiration.

✦ Give back and give thanks. Give away at least 10 percent of your income—and eventually much more, as you become more and more successful.

9. *How to Be Rich*, by J. Paul Getty

⌒ Powerful Millionaire Attitudes ⌒

✦ After Getty made his first million dollars as an independent oil
operator, he retired at the age of twenty-four! He sat around
and did nothing. But his father sat him down and taught him
this: "You've got to use your money to create, operate, and build
businesses. Your wealth represents potential jobs for countless
others—and it can produce wealth and a better life for a great
many people, as well as for yourself." Getty then decided to
come out of retirement at the age of twenty-six!

✦ The door to the American Millionaires Club is not locked. The
person with energy and imagination who can successfully
implement new ideas into new products and services will see
wealth. (In the year 2000, there were 5 million millionaires in
the United States of America. Getty's book was first published
in 1965. So, Getty was right. The American Millionaires Club is
still open and has a wider and more diversified membership
than ever before.)

✦ The "millionaire mentality" is a vitally aware state of mind that
harnesses all of an individual's skills and intelligence to the
goals and tasks of his business.

✦ Getty gives a whole series of business rules of the game that
millionaire business people follow. They cover many areas like:
a solid working knowledge of the business, producing better
products, thrift and self-discipline, recognizing opportunities
for expansion, close and constant supervision of the business,
alertness for new ways to improve the business, and wealth
used as a means to improve living conditions everywhere.

✦ The millionaire mentality must be able to "think small," in the
sense of giving meticulous attention to the smallest details, and
never miss opportunities to reduce costs.

10. *Think and Grow Rich Action Pack,* by Napoleon Hill

◯ **Powerful Millionaire Attitudes** ◯

Below are ten of the great key principles from the prince of all the modern success thinking.

His chief thought as he studied the success formulas of Andrew Carnegie is: Wealth—all achievement, all earned riches—have their beginning in an *idea.* All successful people have these ten keys, as uncovered by Napoleon Hill.

- ✦ A Keen, burning desire to achieve
- ✦ Definiteness of Purpose
- ✦ Faith. Directed faith makes every thought crackle with power.
- ✦ Autosuggestion. Get the deepest part of your mind to go to work for you.
- ✦ Imagination. Imagination is the workshop of your mind, capable of turning energy into accomplishment and wealth.
- ✦ Specialized Knowledge. Knowledge is only *potential* power. It becomes power only when and if it is organized into definite plans of action and directed to an end.
- ✦ Organized Planning. Practice plans that will bring wealth.
- ✦ Decision. Quick, definite decisions are the key that people who have amassed fortunes have in common. People who fail to accumulate money, without exception, have a habit of reaching decisions slowly, if at all, and of changing these decisions quickly and often.
- ✦ Persistence. Persistence is an essential factor in the procedure of transmuting desire into its monetary equivalent. The basis of persistence is the power of will. Willpower and desire, when properly combined, make an irresistible pair. The majority of people are ready to throw their aims and purposes overboard and give up at the first sign of opposition or misfortune. A few carry on, despite all opposition, until they attain their goal.
- ✦ The power of a mastermind group. This is a special advisory group of people who will partner with you for your success.

The advice and encouragement you have received from these success thinkers and financial giants is worth millions of dollars, tons of success, and years of fulfilling living. Pursue these attitudes; then, watch success pursue you.

Powerful Millionaire Attitudes (PMA) from a Well-Known Billionaire of Ancient History

A well-known billionaire has written some great principles about success and about creating and protecting wealth. That billionaire—the ancient king of Israel, King Solomon—lived nearly 3,000 years ago, but his success and wealth-building principles are timeless, current, and powerful. His advice is written in a series of proverbs ascribed to him in the Wealth Book, the Bible. Follow this wise counsel in the Book of Proverbs and you will be successful. I have organized these "Solomon's Wealth-Building PMA" into five sections.

Seventeen More Nuggets of Sound Advice and Attitudes from an Ancient Billionaire

1. Hard Work and Diligence
2. First Things First
3. Doing Your Best
4. Personal Life Issues
5. Wealth and Poverty

King Solomon, the Billionaire

I think I am not being presumptuous in describing Solomon as a *billionaire.* Solomon's exceedingly great prosperity is described in detail in 1 Kings Chapter 10. In verse 14 of Chapter 10, Solomon's revenues from just one business income source was over 250 million dollars a year. This is according to my calculations of modern-day equivalents for the value of 666 talents (about 25 tons) of gold.

KING SOLOMON'S WEALTH-BUILDING PMA

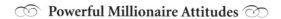

∽ **Powerful Millionaire Attitudes** ∽

1. Hard Work and Diligence

✦ *Hard work means prosperity; only fools idle away their time.*
                                            Proverbs 12:11 (NLT)

✦ *Lazy people want much but get little, but those who work hard will prosper and be satisfied.*
                                            Proverbs 13:4 (NLT)

✦ *The timid become destitute, but the aggressive gain riches.*
                                            Proverbs 11:16 (NRSV)

✦ *All hard work brings a profit, but mere talk leads only to poverty.*
                                            Proverbs 14:23 (NIV)

2. First Things First

✦ *Trust in the LORD with all your heart, and lean not on your own understanding; In all your ways acknowledge Him, and He shall direct your paths.*
                                            Proverbs 3:5–6 (NKJV)

✦ *Honor the LORD with your wealth and with the best part of everything your land produces.*
                                            Proverbs 3:9 (NLT)

✦ *Humility and the fear of the LORD bring wealth and honor and life.*
                                            Proverbs 22:4 (NIV)

3. Doing Your Best

✦ *Do you see a man skilled in his work? He will serve before kings; he will not serve before obscure men.*
                                            Proverbs 22:29 (NIV)

✦ *Do you see a man who excels in his work? He will stand before kings; He will not stand before unknown men.*

Proverbs 22:29 (NKJV)

4. Personal Life Issues

✦ *Fools think they need no advice, but the wise listen to others.*

Proverbs 12:15 (NLT)

✦ *Some pretend to be rich, yet have nothing; others pretend to be poor, yet have great wealth.*

Proverbs 13:7 (NRSV)

✦ *It is better to have little with fear for the LORD than to have great treasure with turmoil. A bowl of soup with someone you love is better than steak with someone you hate.*

Proverbs 15:16,17 (NLT)

5. Wealth and Poverty

✦ *The blessing of the LORD brings wealth, and he adds no trouble to it.*

Proverbs 10:22 (NIV)

✦ *A person who gets ahead by oppressing the poor or by showering gifts on the rich will end in poverty.*

Proverbs 22:16 (NLT)

✦ *He who increases his wealth by exorbitant interest amasses it for another, who will be kind to the poor.*

Proverbs 28:8 (NIV)

✦ *A man who loves wisdom brings joy to his father, but a companion of prostitutes squanders his wealth.*

Proverbs 29:3 (NIV)

✦ *Those who love pleasure become poor; wine and luxury are not the way to riches.*

Proverbs 21:17 (NLT)

I have listed seventy-seven Powerful Millionaire Attitudes. These valuable nuggets of golden truth will empower your thinking and move you forward in your financial life. You are now *without excuse.* Move out now, even if it's only one small step. At least you'll be one step closer to God's best for your life. *Get your thinking right, and the wealth will follow.*

CHAPTER 8

The Second Building Block of Wealth: The Influence of the Community

The Third Building Block of Wealth: The Commitment of the Nation

In this chapter, we will discuss:

✦ The Second Building Block of Wealth: The Influence of the Community

✦ The Seven Habits of a Wealth-Building Community

✦ The Third Building Block of Wealth: The Commitment of the Nation

✦ The Twelve Factors Contributing to the Wealth of Nations

Part One
The Second Building Block of Wealth:
The Influence of the Community

The three building blocks of wealth are again depicted through the visual below. Individuals who practice wealthy attitudes and thinking form strong communities. The communities they develop become the environment and fertile wealth-building communities that are economically empowered and socially attentive. (The second block is now shaded, as it is the subject of our discussion.)

✦ **The Nation (Wealthy Factors)**
✦ **The Community (Wealthy Habits)**
✦ **The Individual (Wealthy Attitudes)**

The Habits of a Wealth-Building Community

Seven Habits of a Wealth-Building Community (a case study)
Modeling a Community's Habits:

The Jewish Phenomenon
Chapter seven discussed seventy-seven Attitudes of Wealth Builders. In it, we heard from individuals who were millionaires and billionaires. We gained insight into the "secrets" (the thinking) of wealthy individuals. The P.I.E.S wealth flow (Producing, Increasing, Enjoying, and Sharing

wealth) works for productive individuals, especially when the environment is also good and conducive to wealth production.

So, the P.I.E.S cycle works for individuals with wealthy thinking, but can it work for a group of people—even an entire race, ethnic group, cultural group, or community? Well, the answer is a resounding, "Yes!" What will work for an individual will work for a people. In this section, we will discover a whole culture (or as some within the group prefer, "tribe") that has developed wealthy habits—the Jewish people.

Modeling the High Achiever

Mark the perfect man, and behold the upright: for the end of that man is peace.

Psalm 37:37(KJV)

A wise man will hear, and will increase learning; and a man of understanding shall attain unto wise counsels.

Proverbs 1:5 (KJV)

Give instruction to a wise man, and he will be yet wiser: teach a just man, and he will increase in learning.

Proverbs 9:9 (KJV)

Let's interpret these verses from a wealth-building perspective: model, emulate, observe, and learn from those who exhibit the positive, empowering wealth-building principles bringing them success. These individuals who model success have learned and perfected the lessons for producing wealth.

The Hebrew word for "mark" in Psalm 37:37 is *shamar,* which means *to observe, keep, and do.* It refers to *watching with intelligence and following the dictates of wisdom, prudence, and justice.* It can imply *to celebrate.* I'm sure you have seen the success of others, but can you also celebrate their success and rejoice in their victory? This Scripture encourages us to observe and celebrate the success in others and to follow their success principles in our own lives.

As humans, we should be joyous when others are successful and be that much more appreciative when those same individuals are willing to share with us the principles that have brought them success. The best selling book *The Millionaire Next Door* opened the eyes of many and inspired them to emulate the millionaire principles and teach these behaviors to their children. The authors, Thomas J. Stanley and William D. Danko, did much research and gave us the millionaire's secrets for success.

Interesting Facts and Statistics

There are over 5 million millionaires in America. However, more staggering is the fact that although Jews make up only 2 percent of the total U.S. population, one-third of all American multimillionaires are Jewish! Want a few more statistics?

+ This Jewish 2 percent of the population makes up 45 percent of the top forty richest Americans.
+ The percentage of Jewish households with annual incomes greater than $50,000 is double that of non-Jews.
+ On the other hand, the percentage of Jewish households with annual incomes less than $20,000 is half that of non-Jews.

These and many other fascinating facts and statistics are revealed in a very helpful and enlightening book by Steven Silbiger, entitled *The Jewish Phenomenon: Seven Keys to the Enduring Wealth of a People* by Longstreet Press. I highly recommend this book for its analysis and information about an oppressed people, who in spite of everything, have succeeded. For me, this is not so much a book about a race (although it is always interesting to read about the human triumph of any people), but it is an insider's *instructional guide* to the thought patterns, behavior, and culture of a wealthy people.

Before any other ethnic groups feel slighted, please know that, as an African American, I understand the challenges and trials of oppression and racial hatred against a people. I love hearing and reading the stories of African Americans who have overcome. Yet, I also appreciate the stories of other peoples who have overcome. So, here in this section, I'm identifying principles of success and wealth that have worked for an ethnic group in America.

Silbiger lists seven principles that he rightly says can be emulated by any group or individual who desires to succeed. Don't envy, emulate. Yes, of course, you will do it with your own personal style, history, and personality, but the Scriptures have counseled us that we will be wiser only if we follow wise principles. So, if you want to be wealthier, listen up. The Father of Faith and Wealth, Abraham, was very wealthy. Listen now to one of his descendents telling us modern day folks about how Abraham's descendants have applied principles that have helped them not only to survive, but also to thrive in an intimidating environment.

About the Book *The Jewish Phenomenon*

This book is about Jewish economic, educational, and social success. It is a book about Jewish development of wealth. But, most of all, it is also a book for all of us. After discussing each of the Seven Keys, Silbiger gives practical hints for implementing these principles into our daily living. Before Silbiger's *Seven Keys to Jewish Success* is listed, let me say that I found a few dominant principles in the book that stood out for me as keys, or prevailing principles.

Six Prevailing Principles of the Book
The Jewish Phenomenon

ONE
For Jews, wealth is a good thing and a worthy and respectable goal for which to strive.
The first Jews were not poor, and Judaism does not consider poverty a virtue.

TWO
Jews have an educational and economic incentive.
Whereas other groups may have athletics, entertainment, or some other

single field as their primary goals, Jews do not. The many other contributions of the Jews to American life and culture are related to their twofold education/economic incentive.

THREE
Jews have the ability to organize and utilize economic strength.
Many other groups may have economic strength but are not able to organize that strength to assist the group in its causes.

FOUR
Jews have a strong, burning entrepreneurial spirit.
Jews have twice the self-employment rate of other ethnic groups. Silbiger says, "This entrepreneurial drive is crucial to Jewish success."

FIVE
Jews are a people of the Book (OT Bible) and a people of books.
Jews are voracious readers. Their purchases are the cornerstone of hardcover book sales, accounting for between 50 percent and 75 percent of sales in the United States.

SIX
For Jews, wealth is a tool for survival.
As Silbiger states, "Without money, Jews view themselves as 'naked to their enemies.'"

Other oppressed groups in America and the world might well pay attention to this belief. It is so similar to the self-empowerment doctrine of Marcus Garvey, who said in his book, *Black Man*: "Wealth is strength, wealth is power, wealth is influence, wealth is justice, is liberty, is real human rights."

Before some of you rise up in disagreement, please observe the fact that the Hebrew words for wealth in the Old Testament define wealth in the same way. The Hebrew words for wealth include the ideas of power and force, or an army. They also mean the strength to do what you want to do. Now, that sounds like wealth! (See Appendix Two for more regarding Hebrew words for wealth.)

The Seven Keys to Jewish Success and Wealth by Steven Silbiger

1. Understand that real wealth is portable; it's knowledge
2. Take care of your own and they will take care of you
3. Successful people are professional and entrepreneurs
4. Develop your verbal confidence
5. Be selectively extravagant but prudently frugal
6. Celebrate individuality: encourage creativity
7. Have something to prove: a drive to succeed

Applying the Seven Keys to the P.I.E.S. Cycle

These principles fit nicely with my P.I.E.S wealth cycle. I have further subdivided the seven keys into nine principles of success and wealth. The results are as follows.

P.I.E.S.
P: Produce Wealth (creating/generating)

1. Real wealth is portable; it's knowledge
Knowledge is the foundation for producing wealth.

2. Be a professional and entrepreneur
These are the occupational types that create wealth.

3. Develop verbal confidence and boldness
This is the inner boldness needed to activate wealth.

Silbiger identifies this skill with the Yiddish word, *chutzpah*, which comes from the Hebrew word meaning "audacity." He refers to Alan Dershowitz's book, *Chutzpah*. The definition of chutzpah is in the following Quotable Quote.

⟆ **A Quotable Quote** ⟆

Definition of *chutzpah*:
Chutzpah—boldness, assertiveness, a willingness to demand what is due, to defy tradition, to challenge authority, to raise eyebrows.
—**Alan Dershowitz**

Chutzpah, do you have it?

4. *Have a drive to succeed*
   This is the tenacity to persist in spite of obstacles. This is an essential key for creating wealth.

5. *Encourage creativity*
   This is the art of independent thinking and daring to be the first to think of or implement a certain process. Thinking "outside the box" characterizes all successful people in any profession.

P.I.E.S.
I: Increase Wealth (preserving/investing)

6. *Be prudently frugal*
   This is the skill and discipline to control your spending habits. It's a much needed key to preserving wealth, so your hard earned wealth does not "sprout wings and fly away."

Regarding the investing aspect of my P.I.E.S. cycle, Silbiger reveals a startling statistic about Jewish investing habits. A reader's survey in *Reform Judaism* showed that a whopping 73 percent of reformed Jews hold stocks and bonds. The average for the general public is 27 percent. Jews have priorities: (1) education, (2) money, (3) material things. He goes on to add, "For Jews, wealth is more than the power to buy things; it is power itself. Money can overcome the prejudices of most bigots, especially in America. . . . In the United States, money breaks down the barriers faster than any pleadings for help."

P.I.E.S.
E: Enjoy Wealth (living/celebrating)

7. *Be selectively extravagant*
   Spend your wealth on the things you desire. Enjoy them, but be selective and not wildly excessive.

8. *Celebrate individuality*
   This is the balance that keeps one sane in the pursuit of work and the struggle to succeed. Enjoy life. Enjoy your wealth. Celebrate who you are. Enjoy being the best you can be.

P.I.E.S.
S: Share Wealth (caring for/empowering others)

9. *Take care of your own and they will take care of you*
   This is the key that allows ethnic and social groups to help themselves and to thereby be freed from an addictive dependency upon outside help.

Silbiger reveals some interesting information about Jews and the care of their own. To safeguard and enhance the community, Jews are zealous in giving their wealth and time for charity and social action. In 1997, Jewish philanthropy totaled 4.5 billion dollars.

Silbiger goes on to say, "In addition, Jews understand that when the community serves itself, it also controls its own destiny. . . . In Judaism, the best donation is the one that aims to create an independent recipient."

This idea is deeply rooted in Jewish religion and society. The twelfth century philosopher Moses Maimonides (Pronounced, mi-MON-neh-deez) determined that there are eight levels of *tzedakah*, which we translate as *charity*. (*Charity, righteousness*, and *justice* all come from the same Hebrew root.) As we stated earlier, the highest level of charity for Maimonides is when, "The person helps another by enabling that person to become self-sufficient through a gift or loan, or helping him gain a skill or find employment."

A Final Silbiger Quote

Silbiger has some advice regarding the need for financial independence for today's workers:

"In the chapter about spending and saving, I made the point that dependent workers, employees, need to create their own capital base. Without capital, employees are at the mercy of their employers to pay their bills. The fear of upsetting the boss prevents employees from being fully creative and productive. If the idea is really such a good one, you can make the big leap with your own capital and pursue your dream yourself. As an entrepreneur, anyone can create real wealth."

P.I.E.S.: A Proven, Time-Tested System

Thus, again the P.I.E.S. cycle is at the foundation of the seven keys of wealth and success for an entire people—the Jews. Isn't that interesting? Especially since I got the P.I.E.S. cycle from their ancient literature (the Old and New Testaments)! Thank God for the P.I.E.S. wealth cycle. It has a proven 4,000-year history of success.

These seven keys and six prevailing principles are rooted in the great American dream—no, in the great human dream. That dream may be different for each of us individually, but as a human quest, that dream is the desire to have a life of purpose and fulfillment, to be the kind of human being that passes on life and love to all that we meet, and to enjoy the political, social, and economic freedom to, "be all that we can be."

Mr. Silbiger, thank you for sharing the seven keys of the enduring wealth of a people.

Note: In another document, I have categorized Silbiger's original list of seven keys into six motivations with seventeen incentives. The motivations can apply to any family, community, or social group. But, if you would like my entire document, which applies these motivations to the economic success of African Americans, go to my coaching Web site, *KenHammonds.com*. The document is entitled *Six Indisputable Keys for the Economic Success of African Americans.*

Part Two:
The Third Building Block of Wealth:
The Commitment of the Nation

⌒ A Quotable Quote ⌒

*A democratic South Africa has opened up avenues for all South
African cultures and religions to prosper and flourish.*
                                              —**President Nelson Mandela**

This quote is from a September 15, 1994, message to Jewish citizens of
South Africa on the occasion of the first celebration of Yom Kippur in a
democratic South Africa.

The Final Building Block of Wealth

The final building block of wealth is the nation. This is as vital as the
other two blocks. They all rise or fall together. Individuals who practice
wealthy attitudes and thinking form strong communities. These communities become the foundation for successful nations that produce
wealth and promote prosperity for their people. Such nations do not
merely give lip service to these ideals but are committed to the wealth of
all peoples within their borders. The three building blocks of wealth are
again depicted through the visual below. (The third block is now shaded, as it is the subject of our discussion.)

✦ **The Nation (Wealthy Factors)**

✦ **The Community (Wealthy Habits)**

✦ **The Individual (Wealthy Attitudes)**

God wants all nations and all peoples of the Earth to be wealthy. God's spiritual and wealth promises to Abraham, Isaac, and Jacob (Israel), and His eternal promise through Jesus Christ were that "all nations" receive the earthly and spiritual blessings. Our prayer should not only be, "God Bless America," but also, "God Bless the World." We are all part of the same Earth and of the same blood. For we know our modern "American" economy is truly a *world economy*, and no nation is an island. We must encourage the enjoyment of honorable wealth building for every citizen of planet Earth, for one nation's poverty will eventually become another nation's problem.

The Wealth and Poverty of Nations

Twelve Factors that Produce Wealth-Building Nations Modeling Nations' Positive Qualities: *The Wealth and Poverty of Nations*

A few years ago, I went to a Web site that listed the books ten of America's top CEOs read. As I looked through the list, a book by Dr. David Landes, History Professor Emeritus of Harvard University, came up several times. This New York Times bestseller was entitled *The Wealth and Poverty of Nations: Why some are so rich and some so poor.* The 600-page paperback seemed as though it would to be too much for me, since it was about history and economics. (Two disciplines that some think to be rather dull.) Landes calls his book a world history, but not in the traditional understanding of the term. His work traces "the main stream economic advance and modernization" of world history.

However, I figured if some of America's best CEOs thought it was worthy reading, I would also give it a try. As it turned out, after I started reading it, I couldn't put it down. I was fascinated by the story the author was telling. Indeed, it was academic and at times challenging reading, but it was also interesting to an economic layman like me. I was delighted to see how beautifully it fit with my P.I.E.S. economic theory of wealth.

Being one who likes things broken down to their most essential elements, I began reading the book, carefully looking at simple ways to reveal the factors contributing to the wealth of nations and the poverty of others. Interestingly enough, I discovered twelve primary factors in the book, and they all start with the letter "C." These factors are not given in the way they are set forth by the author, but rather, are my attempt to simplify the message of this massive work. I didn't look for this order; it just seemed to come out this way. So, below I'll list the twelve critical factors I gleaned from this outstanding 600-page book.

The nations and peoples of the world studied were from the Neolithic Revolution (the latest period of the Stone Age, 8,000 BC to 3,000 BC) to modern day nations. But, the emphasis was from the 1400s to the present day. Landes studies the nations of China, Japan, and the countries of Asia, Africa, Europe, North America, and South America. He also examines the roles of religion and culture in the development of wealth. So, Dr. Landes has thoroughly gleaned the best qualities and factors of wealth-building nations.

Twelve Factors That Produce
Wealth Building Nations

I have divided the twelve primary factors contributing to the wealth of nations into three categories: environmental factors, ideological factors, and business factors.

Environmental Factors of Wealth-Building Nations
(The surrounding physical geography and weather conditions)

1. Climate
2. Crops (cultivation of land, agriculture, and natural resources)

Ideological Factors of Wealth-Building Nations
(The predominate ways a society thinks about itself, its people, and other people)

3. Culture (attitude, values, motivation)
4. Citizens Rights (particularly, property rights and the right to obtain and maintain wealth—the control of their property, both land and wealth)
5. Commitment to Wealth for All (creating/making, getting, spending)

Business Factors of Wealth-Building Nations
(The level of passion and enterprise for developing business ventures and products for profit)

6. Capital (money, or its substitute—a good, educated labor force equals "human capital")
7. Creating Jobs
8. Christian Church (the protestant work ethic: Calvinism or its cultural equivalent. This could be called the industrious revolution)
9. Craftsman of Skill (developing you and developing quality products for the world market)
10. Cultivating Invention (the invention of invention and innovation)
11. Cutting Edge (a research orientation)
12. Commerce (This is enterprise—getting out and doing selling and trading. This forms consumers and competition)

I found these factors can apply to individuals, communities, businesses, and countries. They can benefit from observing these critical principles of wealth-building nations. These twelve factors are essentially God's Wealth Cycle applied to nations.

P: Producing Wealth. Primary Factors 7, 9, 10, 12
I: Increasing Wealth. Primary Factors 2, 6, 11
E: Enjoying Wealth. Primary Factors 1, 3, 8
S: Sharing Wealth. Primary Factors 4, 5

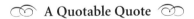

A Quotable Quote

I believe that the time has now arrived for the emergence of a new African. . . . The resources for creating this new man . . . lay within the bosoms of Africa. . . . It is the interaction of the resources within the human person and his surroundings that make for wealth. . . . In turn, the combination of all these factors will stem the tide of scorched-earth exportation of our natural resources.
—Kayode J. Fakinlede, *Wealth of the Yoruba People*

Fakinlede mentions several factors needed to create wealth: a supportive government, utilizing natural and human resources, creating wealth building institutions, forming economic alliances with other ethnic nations, and freedom of determination. These easily fit into categories of the twelve primary factors above. The P.I.E.S. wealth cycle provides the sure foundation for not only personal wealth building but the wealth building of nations, also.

The Wealth Cycle: Good Governments Will Like This Powerful System

Governments will certainly appreciate the P.I.E.S. wealth cycle. (Producing, Increasing, Enjoying, and Sharing wealth). After all, the P.I.E.S. system creates wealth for all and elevates the general citizenry to the status of powerful moneymakers and taxpayers. It is hard to imagine a good government that would fight against the wealth cycle, but I'm sure there are some that consider neither God nor the welfare of the people in their wealth-government equation.

I have listed below some of the benefits the implementation of the P.I.E.S. cycle of wealth can have for governments and governmental agencies that seek to be strong and wealthy. While the list is not complete, it is suggestive of the types of benefits that are inherent in a governmental P.I.E.S. system that frees its people to create wealth. The wealth cycle calls upon self-reliance (in the power of God), not government handouts. The wealth cycle requires individuals to be personally responsible for their actions and especially their own financial well-being. This system does not ask the government to do what the individual should do. The wealth cycle:

1. Decreases poverty and increases the wealth of citizens and other people within the country.
2. Lowers the welfare rolls (in countries that have government welfare).
3. Increases the tax base in both size and scope.
4. Makes for a richer country.

Governments' Responsibilities to the Proper Working of the Wealth Cycle

The Scriptures speak extensively of the responsibilities of governments and governmental leaders to the people they serve. It is not our purpose here to go into depth in this discussion but to merely list the issues and responsibilities. If governments foster a healthy and beneficial social order, if governments promote an environment of peace and prosperity, and if governments provide for the safety of all residents, the people *will* produce the wealth. My suggestions are below:

1. Governments should not place a heavy burden of taxation upon the people. Excessive taxes inhibit the activation of the P.I.E.S. system.
2. Governments are to respect the personal property, including the land rights, of the people.
3. Governments are not to unjustly place servitude, bondage, or imprisonment upon the people for their own selfish motives or for the personal pleasures of those in leadership.
4. Governmental leaders are to be examples of personal control and responsibility.
5. Governmental leaders should take an oath of office that obligates them to serve the people and not themselves.
6. Governmental leaders are to fear God.

Social and economic justice (right actions and proper behavior) by governments are essential to the working of the wealth cycle. Wealth cannot be fully released among the people where there is a governmental system that does not encourage the release of the wealth builder within its citizenry. Any nation that does not seek the good (peace and prosperity) of its people will incur the displeasure of God, the wrath of the people, and will eventually sow the seeds of its own demise.

The P.I.E.S. wealth cycle is a wonderful system for changing lives and shaping the world. God has given us the perfect system for carrying out His plan for human development and civilization's progress. When we observe God's Wealth Cycle, we'll be better equipped to see some of the difficulties of society disappear and each individual, family, community, and society-at-large grow and reach its economic potential.

The Building Blocks of Wealth: Conclusion

The building blocks of wealth—the individual (attitudes), the community (habits), and the nation (factors)—together are powerful forces for building wealth in human society. Consider all the powerful attitudes (seventy-seven), habits (seven), and factors (twelve) wealth builders have left for us to follow. As motivational speaker, Tony Robbins says, "Success leaves clues." And those who have created, shaped, and distributed the wealth of the world have also left "ninety-six clues," and I'm sure there are more. But, even *one* of these clues fully believed and carried out with prayer, a positive attitude, and persistence will change your financial future and your life.

Our pioneering wealth builders have paved the way on the road to wealth. And in today's world, more than at any other time in human history, the road to wealth has widened and carries travelers from all races, ethnic groups, social classes, and communities around the world. Thank you, wealth builders, for leaving a blueprint for any of us to utilize as we build wealth in our lives. It is just as J. Paul Getty has said, "The door to the American [or world] Millionaires Club is not locked. The person with energy and imagination who can successfully implement new ideas into new products and services will see wealth." Do you have a God-idea that will take you on a journey on the road to wealth and move you upward on the Wealth Continuum?

Note: People with expertise in political theory, social systems, etc., can further work out the details of the meaning of the wealth cycle and the responsibilities of government. I trust I have tilled a fertile soil in which many will plant. I will personally expound Biblically and philosophically on these in a discussion oriented Web site called *WealthTheology.com* to be formed in the fall of 2004. If you might be interested in contributing to the content and discussion of this Web site, please contact me at my email address, *KH@WealthyThinking.com,* or call me at 323-753-1366 for more information.

PART FOUR

Taking Action

 A KH Question

Wake up and smell the money!

*In your wealth building life, are you an
action figure or a sleeping giant?*

*All hard work brings a profit, but mere talk leads only to
poverty.*

Proverbs 14:23 (NIV)

CHAPTER 9

The Challenge of Wealth's Enemies

In this short chapter, we will discuss:

✦ **Four Enemies of Wealth and Success**

(Read and ponder carefully. These four enemies are the reasons why wealth and success are not experienced by every human being on the planet.)

Four Enemies of Wealth and Success

∽ A Quotable Quote ∾

*"Terrorism really flourishes in areas of poverty,
despair, and hopelessness, where people see no future."*
—**Colin Powell**

*I*n Part One, I boldly stated that God designed the human race for wealth and success and that you were born for wealth in every area of life. I went so far as to declare that wealth is the natural human condition. I even declared poverty, or lack, is an aberration, an abnormality, and a deviation from God's wealth standard. In Part Two, we discussed how to release the powerful wealth builder within. And in Part Three, we established the essential building blocks of wealth where we get the right attitudes, habits, and discover the right factors for building wealth and success in the individual, the community, and the nation.

Well, if this is true, and humans have all this support for success and wealth around them, one might rightfully ask, "So, what challenges and stifles the release of the inner wealth builder? What causes poverty, lack, and limits the flow of wealth from God to humankind? If all this talk about a Divine Wealth Cycle is true, what then hinders the activation and continuous movement of the wealth cycle? Why isn't everyone wallowing in wealth, or at least getting by?"

The answer to these puzzling questions is simple, yet profound: four enemies. There are two internal enemies and two external enemies of wealth and success. Wealth, success, and blessings *do* have enemies. Even God Himself has enemies.

This chapter presents the reason everyone is not enjoying abundance and wealth, the reason why there are the *haves* and the *have nots*—it is because of the four enemies. These enemies limit success and hinder the spread of wealth throughout the Earth. I'm identifying these enemies so we might avoid them, attack them, radically reduce them, or eliminate their devastating influence in human affairs. Many Bible teachers have identified three enemies: this world's system dominated by evil, the sinful desires within humans, and the personification of evil, the Devil (commonly identified as the world, the flesh (sin nature), and the Devil). I've added a fourth—YOU!

The Four Enemies:
+ Sin
+ Satan
+ Systems
+ Self-Imposed Limitations

When this chapter regarding the enemies of wealth and success is developed with other principles in the rest of this book, you'll clearly see why all God's creatures unfortunately don't enjoy the abundance for which they were created. You will also discover how to destroy the four enemies by developing wealthy thinking and actions that bring results.

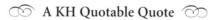 A KH Quotable Quote

Since God is therefore the source of wealth,
who then would be the source of poverty?

Enemy #1: Sin
An Internal Enemy

Sin, the part of human nature that seeks only selfishness and self-will, is an enemy of success. There is a nature within the human heart that seeks self above all: self-pleasure, self-service, self-love, and self-ambitions—all at the expense of another's health and welfare. We humans have a vast capacity for greed, hatred, prejudice, divisiveness, murder, wrath, lewdness of conduct, lying, idolatry (some even regarding themselves or their systems as if they were God), sexual perversion, inflicting of pain and suffering on other humans, and many other personally and socially destructive activities.

These are the effects of this inner disposition and powerfully negative stench called sin. This is the number-one enemy of success and wealth. Sin exists within all economic, racial, and social classes of human cultures.

Enemy #2: Satan
An External Enemy

Satan has a clearly focused activity and plan here on Earth. He approaches us and advances his active attack upon humans to steal, kill, and destroy that which can be productive for the work of God and betterment of human society.

Satan is the great adversary (opposer, resister) of the people of God and of people who are trying to do good. Also noteworthy is the fact that the NT word translated as "Devil" is the Greek word *diabolos*. *Diabolos* is the word from which we get our English word, "diabolical." Its verbal form means *to be set in opposition, to accuse, to slander, to give false information.*

So, the Devil gives people false information about themselves, the situation they are in, and what to do to get out. Ever had an "inner voice" speak loudly to you, accusing you of being dumb, stupid, or ugly? Does that voice also tell you that everyone hates you or that you are just plain lousy? That's the Devil. Yes, he is a strong opponent of true success. Satan is an enemy of wealth. He spreads pain, suffering, oppression, and poverty.

Enemy #3: Systems
An External Enemy

Two formidable foes have been listed above as enemies of success and wealth, but there is another that is extremely powerful and can continue when the humans who originally created it are no longer around. That third enemy is systems—unhealthy or evil human systems. There are numerous human systems, and all have the potential for hindering or destroying human wealth, health, success, freedom, and joy.

Some human systems have been hostile to God and God's way. Examples of such human systems are: governments, religions, political parties, slavery systems, discriminatory systems (racism, classism, sexism, segregation), intellectual/philosophical systems (various views on issues which become systematized and presented as truth), families, and educational institutions.

Some of these systems have great potential for promoting the human good, but they all have a history of hindering the wealth God intended for every human being. Many human systems actually *cause* the poverty, pain, sickness, or death of their own members and creators, usually through greed. Systems like governments, schools, religions, and some families should cease hindering their citizens and the people of those systems from enjoying true wealth. If every human system followed God's Wealth Cycle, every facet of society would experience greater benefits.

Enemy #4: Self-Imposed Limitations An Internal Enemy

⌒⌒ A Quotable Quote ⌒⌒

If we all did the things we are capable of doing,
we would literally astound ourselves.

—**Thomas Edison**

The last enemy of success is perhaps the most powerful of them all, and the most difficult to defeat. It is the hindrance of self-imposed limitations. This is the great nemesis of the ages and the most personal enemy: the enemy within. The great cartoon philosopher Pogo Possum said, "We have met the enemy, and he is us!"

This is the enemy that stops most of us. It's not so much the "system" or "those people" or "them folks." It's the "man in the mirror" who holds you back, especially in the United States of America. And it's also true for the believer in the God of abundance.

We are people of success and victory. The only limits are those we set for ourselves. Self-mastery through the power of God can defeat any enemy. The Scriptures say in 1 John 4:4 (KJV), *greater is he that is within you than he that is within the world.* It is you who finally decides to let sin reign in your life, thereby destroying your body, soul, and spirit. It is you who decides to let Satan rob you of your wealth birthright. It is you who decides to let some system destroy the reason you were created. It's not others who ultimately decide our fate. It is our decisions that shape the wealth or lack of wealth in our lives. It's not the freedom given to you by someone else or by some system that sets you free—it's the freedom from within.

Yes, these four enemies of success limit or stop the flow of God's Wealth Cycle. For the rest of this chapter, let's focus upon what you can do to avoid being restricted and perhaps destroyed by the greatest enemy of all—self-imposed limitations.

An Example from Human History

Think of the beginnings of the enslaved African in the United States. Yes, the black man has had a rough American beginning. Yes, even a bad, bitter, battered beginning. Our families were divided; our women were sexually abused and raped; we were unmercifully whipped, beaten, murdered; and as a people, we were deemed less than human—only mere property. (In early America, Blacks were said to be only three-fifths of a human being. And they were considered only that much of a human being for legislative purposes, for the official population census in the southern states.) But, despite all that, there was a *divine destiny*.

Similarly, perhaps you too (no matter what your ethnic, social, or economic background) may have also had a bad, bitter, battered beginning in life. However, each of us has a divine destiny. Will you fulfill your destiny, or will you be satisfied with being bound in your mind? Will you let self-limitations hold back the promise of God? Remember, we are overcomers.

A great example of someone refusing to be defeated by self-imposed limitations is Madam C. J. Walker (1867–1919), an entrepreneur, hair-care industry pioneer, philanthropist, social activist, and the first African American woman millionaire. She was voted as *Black Enterprise* magazine's, "Entrepreneur of the 20th Century." Her personal achievements and her experience of freedom came from within despite the "system" that was against her.

+ She was married at age fourteen, but her husband died, leaving her with a two-year old daughter.
+ She taught herself to read and write.

- ✦ She started with $1.25, determination, a dream, and never looked back.
- ✦ She was the first to sell products by mail order.
- ✦ She was a millionaire who lived in the super-affluent mansion neighborhood of the Vanderbilts and other rich families.
- ✦ At the National Negro Business League Convention, July 1912, she said, "I am a woman who came from the cotton fields of the South. From there I was promoted to the washtub. From there I was promoted to the cook kitchen. And from there I promoted myself into the business of manufacturing hair goods and preparations... I have built my own factory on my own ground."
- ✦ She also said, "I got myself a start by giving myself a start."
- ✦ She has a strong word today for those who face any kind of difficulty working on their dream. Her advice to women at the National Negro Business League in 1912 was a business philosophy that stressed economic independence for women: "I want to say to every Negro woman present, don't sit down and wait for the opportunities to come. . . .Get up and make them!"

Now that's freedom from within!

Stop your excuses for not being all God has called you to be. Recognize the freedom within you!

Common Self-Limiting Thoughts and Talk

Below is a list of some negative, self-defeating statements. Have you ever said or thought any of these or something similar? All the statements below can be characterized as *stinkin' thinkin'.*

- ✦ I am afraid.
- ✦ I have nothing to offer.
- ✦ What I have to offer is so small it will make no difference.
- ✦ I've been working hard and don't see any results yet. I quit.

+ I have no one to help me.
+ Blame the woman or the man who is in your life (or who *was* in your life).
+ Blame someone else: the Devil or maybe even God.
+ The dog ate my homework.
+ I can't.
+ They are stronger than I am.
+ I don't have any money.
+ I'm a failure.
+ I feel like a grasshopper in my own eyes. (See Numbers 13:30–14:2. This was the response of Israel to the challenges before them when they faced the giants in the land God promised to them. Their response was that of fear rather than faith.)
+ I can't find funding, so I give up.
+ Who am I? I'm a nobody.
+ I wish I were dead.
  (But, the answer to your problems and challenges is not in the request to die; it's the resolve to live—to become *fully alive*. A new level of living brings with it a new level of joy in the present, even in the midst of seeming failure.)

When all else fails, we disrespectfully ask God for a world exit. All of us have felt this way at some time in our lives. Even the great prophet Elijah was in fear after his greatest spiritual victory and said to the Lord, "Take my life." The answer for him was food, rest, meditation, prayer, and the consolation of God's Presence. Maybe that's the prescription for you, too.

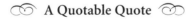

A Quotable Quote

Our deepest fear is not that we are inadequate.
Our deepest fear is that we are powerful beyond measure.
                                        —**Marianne Williamson**

Mental Barriers that Limit Wealth

Below is a listing of some mental barriers that limit success.

- ✦ Fear of being wealthy
- ✦ Fear of failure (afraid to attempt to be wealthy)
- ✦ Fear of losing wealth
- ✦ A scarcity mentality
- ✦ Ignorance of how money works
- ✦ Feeling undeserving of wealth when others are poor
- ✦ Not believing you are smart enough to be wealthy
- ✦ Believing you are too poor to be wealthy
- ✦ Misunderstanding God's plan for the wealth of the world
- ✦ Unrealized personal potential
- ✦ To summarize the above: A poverty mentality

Wealthy Thinking

The self-limiting thinking and the mental barriers to success listed above come from a poverty mentality. As we would suspect, the poverty mentality is the opposite of a wealthy mentality or wealthy thinking. So, in this section, we will list and analyze wealthy thinking and poverty mentality. Since thinking is the catalyst for action, certainly understanding proper thinking will assist us in developing the right kind of thinking to support the success we desire.

Definition of Poverty Mentality

A *poverty mentality* is non-productive, fearful, and negative thinking. Rather than producing wealth, the poverty mentality destroys it and thereby lowers the level of human existence—for the individual, the community, and the nation.

Wealthy Thinking: A Three-Fold Definition

1. Wealthy thinking is a spiritual attitude or mindset of abundance, prosperity, productivity, wholeness, and growth. It emphasizes the balance of spiritual, material, and relational wealth and well-being.

2. Wealthy thinking also emphasizes the personal development of wealth-producing resources within for the fulfillment of mission and purpose.

3. And lastly, wealthy thinking promotes prosperity and successful living for all.

Wealthy thinking produces abundant living. I say, "Get your thinking right, and the wealth will follow."

Wealthy Thinking: A Shorter Definition

Wealthy thinking is a spiritual attitude of abundance and productivity.

Defining Wealthy Thinking by Contrasts

The opposite of wealthy thinking is a poverty mentality, which sets its mind upon lack, negativity, fearfulness, and non-productive or destructive behaviors. Poverty thinking destroys wealth. Actually, it brings utter annihilation because poverty thinking also destroys even the possibility of wealth.

Poverty thinking says: "There's no way (lack) to do it, and I won't even look for one (fear, non-productivity)."

Ordinary thinking says: "There might be a way (limited to one or a few) to do it, but I can't find it (lack of drive)."

Wealthy thinking says: "There are many ways (abundance) it can be done, and I will find out how (strong-minded action)."

Wealthy thinking is not ordinary human thinking. It is extra-ordinary, above-normal thinking, producing abundant results from the fruit of its labor.

The key to defeating self-limiting thinking and mental barriers is to exercise wealthy thinking. However, wealthy thinking will not only defeat this enemy of wealth and success, it will defeat any foe, for wealthy thinking is God's Spirit working in the human mind to bring prosperity to the world.

The Spirit of Fear

For God has not given us a spirit of fear but of power and of love and of a sound mind.

2 Timothy 1:7 (NKJV)

And he saith unto them, Why are ye fearful, O ye of little faith? Then he arose, and rebuked the winds and the sea; and there was a great calm.

Matthew 8:26 (KJV)

In the two verses above, the words translated *fear* and *fearful* are the Greek words, *deilias* (day-LEE-as), and *deilos* (day-LOS) which mean *cowardly, timidly, fearful,* or *fainthearted.* In their more negative sense, these words also refer to those who are *worthless, poor, miserable, unfortunate,* and *without luck* (*unlucky*).

Fearful (full of fear), cowardly (*deilos*) kinds of thinkers believe they are simply *unlucky* and that successful people have gotten where they are by *being lucky.* And, they are the unfortunate ones whose lives are tossed about by the winds and waves of fate. This Greek word (*deilos*) in its plural form carries the force of, "Those poor folks!"

But Paul told Timothy in 2 Timothy 1:7 that God has not given us a, "poor me" attitude. This attitude says, "I'm just unlucky," "I'm timid about pursuing God's best," or "I'm worthless."

In Matthew Chapter 8, Jesus had to question his own disciples about their belief in him and God when they were in a raging storm while crossing the Sea of Galilee in a boat. He said, "Why do you think you are so unfortunate and unlucky (*deilos*)?" (They had declared, "We're all going to die!"—even though Jesus already told them they would arrive safely to the other side of the lake in the boat.)

So, for all you poor, fearful, *unlucky folks,* I have seven quotes to rid your mind of those lucky and unlucky thoughts. (Yes, seven, so you can feel lucky!)

Seven Quotable Quotes:

1. *I'm a great believer in luck, and I find the harder I work the more I have of it.*

   —Thomas Jefferson

2. *The man who is intent on making the most of his opportunities is too busy to bother about luck.*

   —B.C. Forbes

3. *Luck is what a capricious [lazy] man believes in.*

   —Benjamin Disraeli

4. *The champion makes his own luck.*

   —Red Blaik

5. *Luck is largely a matter of paying attention.*

   —Susan M. Dodd

6. *Luck is what you have left over after you give 100 percent.*

   —Langston Coleman

7. *Shallow thinkers believe in luck; wise, strong, and spiritual people believe in God and work.*

   —KH

Remember this: Success favors the bold.

Get rid of unproductive, negative, fearful thinking—replacing it with the knowledge that God's power is working inside you. Only when you allow His power to work in you will you begin to powerfully shape and mold your future.

Your potential in God is untapped and truly unlimited.
Remember, there are no limits in God.
Limit? What Limit? Go for it!
God is the Limit!

Just as limitation is natural for humans, omnipotence is natural for God.

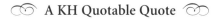 A KH Quotable Quote

*Place no preconceived limitations upon yourself, because when
you limit yourself, you also limit God's ability to work through you.*

DO YOU BELIEVE?

A History of the Word "Believe"

The history of the modern English word believe reveals that it is a combination of two words *be* and *lieve**. The root word *lieve* was originally
Latin. *Lieve* meant: to hold dear, care for, or to love. The usage of the
prefix *be* here is referred to as an intensive prefix. It emphasizes any
word to which it is attached

So, first of all, to believe literally means to care strongly about something with a firm certainty. It is to be passionate about something.
Having a trust, certainty, and passion, which bring a firm conviction—
that's belief. In fact, the NT Greek word for believe, *pisteuō*, adds the
element of making a commitment.

Putting this all together, then clarifies to believe as meaning to trust
with **firm certainty** and therefore **to commit oneself with passion** to a
person, system, or idea. Like its counterpart, love, real belief is always
followed up with action.

So, are you *really* a believer?
Is there anything you are *passionately committed* to?

Jesus Christ said, *"Everything is possible for him who believes."* (Mark
9:23, NIV)

THE BELIEVER'S WORLD IS A WORLD OF POSSIBILITIES

* The basic etymological information for the word "believe" is from The American
  Heritage Dictionary of the English Language, Internet Web site.

CHAPTER 10

Five Action Steps for a Life of Wealth Building

In this chapter, we will discuss:

✦ This Book's Conclusion: Twelve P.I.E.S. Affirmations
✦ Action Steps You Can Take Right Now
✦ A Call to Commitment

How to Design a Life of True Wealth and Abundance

$\mathcal{S}$o then, how does an individual who needs empowerment in her or his situation actually design a life of true wealth and abundance? The answer is commitment to action. You must be a person of action and commitment to producing multi-dimensional wealth.

God Wants You to be Wealthy has presented a complete theory and system with several ideas, hints, and strategies for designing a life that will build and enjoy God's wealth and abundance. Now that you have completed reading the chapters, declared affirmations to yourself, you are well on the way toward enjoying God's best for your life.

However, to experience change in your life, the inspiration and strategies must be put into action. The categories that follow, regarding the twelve affirmations, action steps, commitment to success agreement, and empowering meditation will assist you in laying out a plan for designing your life.

A Call to Commitment

Now that you have read about God's Wealth Cycle, it is time to make a commitment. Commitment to success precedes the experience of success. A true commitment is an *obligation of one's total self to some action, person, or belief.* Are you willing to make a full commitment to living in God's wealth and living the disciplines required to build it? This pledge is first and foremost to God, then to living the Word, and finally, to persistent adherence to the P.I.E.S. cycle. With passionate commitment, you can achieve any goal, overcome any obstacle, or defeat any enemy.

One of you [with commitment] puts to flight a thousand, since it is the LORD your God who fights for you, as he promised you. Be very careful, therefore, to love the LORD your God.

Joshua 23:10–11 (NRSV)

This Book's Conclusion In Twelve Wealth-Building Affirmations

Well, we have covered much in this wealth commentary. How about a conclusion condensing this into twelve affirmations? These twelve wealth-building affirmations are designed to release renewed thinking, joyous living, and personal wealth into your life. These affirmations declare who you are and who you will become.

Produce Wealth (P)
+ I am a natural born producer of wealth. I was born to be a producer, not merely a consumer.
+ I think maximum wage—not minimum wage.
+ I turn opportunity into money, and my wealth flows from multiple sources of income.

Increase Wealth (I)
+ I am a monetary genius. I invest wisely, save diligently, and spend frugally.
+ I am 100 percent committed to avoiding waste and avoiding debt.
+ I am 100 percent committed to living below my means.

Enjoy Wealth (E)
+ I know that God has given me this world and universe to enjoy.

✦ I will have an attitude of gratitude and praise in all I do. I can and will celebrate.

✦ Every problem has a Divine solution.

Share Wealth (S)

✦ I give abundantly and God multiplies it back to me many fold.

✦ I freely open doors of opportunity for others and joyously observe the doors also opening for me.

✦ Money is good—very good. The more money I have, the more influence I have, and the more good I can do.

Five Action Steps You Can Take Right Now

So, after reading about what God says in His Book, what others say in their books, and what I say in my book about building wealth, what will you say about *your* power to create wealth and apply God's Wealth Cycle to your life? In this chapter, we will bring together the many elements of this book and assist you placing your strategy in clear steps. The four steps discussed in the rest of this chapter will advance your calling as a wealth builder.

FIRST: Repeat often and write this on a card or piece of paper, "God wants me to be wealthy!" Place this card in a place that will keep you in remembrance of your declaration (the bathroom mirror, refrigerator, computer screen, etc.).

SECOND: Select seven Scriptures from the various chapters of this book that especially speak to you, which you will commit to memory and meditation. God's Word must be in your heart, not just on the pages of the Bible. Then write down these verses, post them wherever you can see them, and constantly be reminded of God's promises to you.

THIRD: Return to Chapter 7, and note what others have said about the millionaire mentality. Pick seven PMA (Powerful Millionaire Attitudes) you need to develop or be reminded of at this stage of your life.

Write these seven PMA principles down and place them on one sheet of paper. Call these *Keys for Bringing Wealth into My Life.* Review them daily. Live by them. When it seems, after several weeks of application, that these seven keys are an active part of your mind and life, then add more. Keep on adding your new success keys to your list until you get to thirty. This is now your monthly success keys list. Review one key every day to remind yourself of who you are and who you are becoming.

In a few months, you will not only have these thirty keys on paper, but you will be forming many personal disciplines for true wealth and success in your life. You will see the difference and achieve things in your life that you never before thought were possible.

FOURTH: Make a commitment to teach the P.I.E.S. cycle and wealth-building principles to others. Teach your children, your entire family, your friends, your neighbors, your Bible study group—everyone and everywhere. What is their special need? You can assist them. Want to know how to present P.I.E.S. to others? Some practical ways are listed below. I'll give a life situation followed by a suggested P.I.E.S. response. Of course, these are only examples. I'm sure as you practice P.I.E.S. and begin talking more about these life-changing principles, you will see many more applications to daily living.

Note: If you would be interested in starting or being a part of an official G'W Study-Fellowship Group that meets monthly in your area, please contact me for more information. Each study-fellowship group will discuss various principles and strategies of G'W and the application of these principles to the lives of the participants. You can contact me at 323-753-1366, or email me at KH@WealthyThinking.com.

Situation #1: Are They in a Cycle of Debt or Poverty?

P.I.E.S. Response: Let them know they *can* help break this cycle through the power of God. Share the positive affirmations and success quotes of this book. Then, you, too, must positively affirm them, pray with them, and pray for them. Present the appropriate Scriptures and ideas of the "P" of the P.I.E.S. cycle and the practical ideas for producing wealth in Chapter 4. Have them read Chapter 3 about the story of the single, "untalented" woman in 2 Kings Chapter 4, and work with them to discover the

God-hidden talent within. (Don't let them get away with saying, "I have no talent." God has given everyone some special gift or ability.)

Situation #2: Do They Only Have a Small Amount of Resources?

P.I.E.S. Response: Challenge them to preserve and increase "I"— what they do have. Encourage them not to lose it through waste and misman-agement. Review the section in Chapter 5 about increasing wealth.

Also, make the saving of money and resources a game and fun. Brainstorm with the individual about ways to save money using coupons, sales, special events, buying in bulk, etc. Have her or him keep up with spending by keeping a detailed list of expenditures. Though sav-ing is extremely important, it is still important to also work with the per-son to produce more income. See the section above.

Situation #3: Are They in Need of Your Resources for Help in Their Situation?

P.I.E.S. Response: You can share your resources with them. This is the "S" of the cycle in which you can directly become involved. You should reread Chapter 5's section on Sharing Wealth.

Situation #4: They Have Heard It Before. Now They Want to See It Work in You.

P.I.E.S. Response: You can share P.I.E.S and these powerful wealth-build-ing principles with anyone. Yes, talk it up. Nevertheless, you can best teach a wealth-building lifestyle by living it. You can inspire and influ-ence others by personally living a life of abundance and joy. This is the "E" of the wealth cycle. Wealthy living incarnate (in the flesh) is the only way anyone will know for sure the principles of P.I.E.S. do work.

FIFTH: Make your own personal commitment to wealth building in every area of life. Take the call to commitment seriously (see below) and be deter-mined to achieve all God has for you in this life. Get a wealth-building plan (perhaps starting with a home-based business) and work it diligently.

THE COMMITMENT TO SUCCESS AGREEMENT

Review this once a week for a year, then renew it annually.

I, _____ , do hereby give my will to God the Father. I will submit myself totally to the Lordship of Jesus Christ and His Word in every area of life. I will do this through the power of Jesus Christ in me and the renewal of the Spirit.

I commit myself prayerfully and thoughtfully as I sign this Commitment to Success Agreement. It is a covenant between God and me, and between me and myself. It is my personal covenant to a life of PMA (Powerful Millionaire Attitudes)—to think and live wealth and success.

I give myself to the release of wealth and the flow of God's Wealth Cycle. I will seek true wealth and success by being active in pursuing the P.I.E.S cycle and multi-dimensional wealth. I will fully activate the empowerment principles of spiritual and economic wealth building (wealthy thinking and wealthy habits) to release personal, social, and economic prosperity into my life.

_____   _____

YOUR SIGNATURE   DATE

To make your mental assent to the disciplines of wealth and success a real part of your life, prayerfully and thoughtfully sign this Commitment to Success Agreement. It is between you and God, and between you and yourself. It is your personal covenant to a life of Producing, Increasing, Enjoying, and Sharing wealth.

Yes, the commitment is to pursue harmony in the four areas of the P.I.E.S. cycle. However, in order for us to achieve success, we must be specific in our application of the cycle. In the Application section below, please list the specific needs in the P.I.E.S. cycle to which you will make a commitment. If you wish to produce a better spiritual relationship to God, you might list things like: Bible reading and study, fasting, consistent prayer life, etc. If you wish to produce more financial wealth in your life, include the ways you can produce wealth. Make a full commitment to the process.

The P.I.E.S. cycle can activate success in every area of your life—personal, spiritual, relationships, career, and financial stability—and you can apply it to any area of life that you choose. However, please also make some clear financial goals, because as we have now realized, material, emotional, and relational wealth are all a part of God's desire.

Please be honest and seek to find specific needs to enhance your life. They might be for control of temper, a lifestyle of stability, renewing your marriage, pledging greater commitment to your family, going back to school, consistent savings, reducing debt *forever*, etc. No matter what your commitment, make sure you review your commitments weekly. Remain focused during this year-long (indeed, life-long) commitment.

I suggest you assess your progress and future direction by renewing and amending your Commitment to Success Agreement annually. But, for best results, review it and update it at least quarterly. If you wish to have some *personal coaching* in any area please contact me directly or visit my Web site *KenHammonds.com* for information about various personal or group coaching sessions being offered.

A KH Quotable Quote

Focused Focus
Specific focus brings specific results;
Haphazard focus brings haphazard results;
No focus brings no results.

How focused is your focus?

The Application of P.I.E.S
Your Specific Commitments Toward
Richly Enjoying Your Life

Step One: Make a Commitment

Commitment to Produce (Create/Generate) Wealth:
Please list the specific ways you will begin to produce wealth in your life.

_____ _____

_____ _____

_____ _____

Commitment to Increase (Preserve and Invest) Wealth:
Please list the specific ways you will begin to preserve, save, and invest the wealth in your life.

_____ _____

_____ _____

_____ _____

Commitment to Enjoy (Really Living and Celebrating) Wealth:
Please list the specific ways you will begin to enjoy and celebrate the wealth already in your life. Find any excuse you can to celebrate the big and the little victories and the special occasions in your life.

_____ _____

_____ _____

_____ _____

Commitment to Share (Care for and Empower Others with) Wealth:
Please list the specific ways you will begin to share the wealth in your life with others.

_____   _____

_____   _____

_____   _____

Step Two: Work on Specific Goals

Now, from the list above, choose the most important four things you can make a 100 percent commitment to, for as long as it takes to get each item completed. If you can, try working on one item from each area of P.I.E.S. And if you must, break a big or long-term goal into specific, smaller steps so you can see each movement toward success.

1. _____

2. _____

3. _____

4. _____

When any item is completed, return to step one above (your P.I.E.S. commitments), to place another item on this list. Before you know it, you will complete all your commitments and be well on your way toward wealth and success.

Note: A more complete application of the P.I.E.S. system, called a P.I.E.S. chart, is available at *WealthyThinking.com* or *KenHammonds.com*. The P.I.E.S. chart assists you in setting goals in twelve areas of your life.

An Empowering Meditation

This chapter, and perhaps the entire book, can be condensed to the application of the statement below. Please meditate upon this declaration and its meaning for you. Be empowered to live by it daily.

A KH Quotable Quote

Refuse to be less than God has created you to be.

+ What does that statement mean to you?
+ Have you given up on your dreams?
+ What excuses have you given God and others as to why you have refused to aggressively pursue and develop God's gifts, talents, skills, and Calling in you?

I have no greater joy than to see the people of God's planet living in the joy and power of God's true wealth and their God-ordained purpose on Earth.

I know the problems on this Earth are powerful and many, but I also know our spiritual weapons are all-powerful and abundant. I am fully persuaded that godly wealth building—embracing the compatibility of spirituality and wealth and linking them in spiritual harmony, and pursuing God's Wealth Cycle of Producing, Increasing, Enjoying, and Sharing Wealth—is the solution to many of our spiritual, material, and relational ills.

> **I trust this wealth commentary has made you richer—richer because it has reminded you of the great riches you already possess.**

AN INVITATION
A Personal Invitation to
Spiritual Wealth

CO This Invitation CO
This little message is for anyone who wishes to advance his or her spiritual life and receive full spiritual, eternal life in God.

Beginning Enhanced Spiritual Life

I'm sure you know by now that Jesus Christ said he came to give abundant life. Well, that abundance is not just material. If it were, it would be limited, temporary, shallow, and ultimately empty. The pursuit of things cannot fill the spiritual soul deep within. If you have never considered spiritual life in Jesus or if you are no longer active in your spiritual life, just think and pray about the points in this chapter.

The steps are simple; but once taken, your life will be full of excitement, inner joy, and challenge. These steps will challenge your thinking, self-centeredness, and daily living, but they will also give you the greatest hope a human can have—eternal, spiritual life in God and the promise of God's presence and power every day of your life.

Please don't just skip over this because you have experienced some problems with a church. It's not about church people—it's about your spiritual life. So, consider the message below. If you have any further questions about this BIG spiritual life issue, please contact me and I'll be happy to discuss this with you.

I would like to personally invite you to enjoy a new level of life in God. I call this Invitation, "Seven Steps to True Spiritual Wealth."

Special thanks to Pastor Bob Jackson of Oakland, California. His "Ten Step Witnessing Plan" has laid the foundation for my Seven Steps Approach.

Seven Steps to True Spiritual Wealth

Step One: Consider this Good News

Dear Friend,
I trust you have enjoyed reading this wealth book and putting many of its principles into action in your life. But, just for a few moments, I'd like to invite you to consider some Good News I'm telling people about success.

Did you know, *God wants you to be wealthy?* . . . Well, He does! He loves you and wants you to enjoy wealth in EVERY area of your life –spiritually, financially, physically, in your personal relationships with people, in everything in your life now, and in your future.

Step Two: Believe God Wants You to Live Abundantly

Did you know the Bible says the living God has richly and abundantly given us everything in this life to enjoy?

Did you know the Bible says the living God has richly and abundantly given us everything in this life to enjoy? (1 Timothy 6:17)

Again, the Bible says, *Beloved, I pray that you may prosper in all things and be in health, just as your soul prospers* (3 John 1:2).

So, let me ask you: do you believe that? I'm sure you do because you want the best for your life.

Step Three: Believe God Wants You to be Spiritually Wealthy

Did you also know God wants your life to be full of success?

Do you believe this, too? I'm sure you know the first success God wants for us is spiritual wealth. For the Bible says to be spiritually wealthy, you must *confess with your mouth the Lord Jesus and believe in your heart that God has raised Him from the dead; you will be saved* (Romans 10:9).

That word "saved" means to have spiritual freedom and wealth in God through His Son, Jesus Christ.

Step Four: Confess that Jesus is the Lord of Spiritual Wealth

The foundation of that spiritual life is the plan of God in sending Jesus to die for our sins and to be raised from the dead for our spiritual life of abundance. Our sins are our spiritual and moral failures before God, others, and ourselves.

Can you say, "Jesus is the Lord of spiritual wealth in God"? Say that out loud now, if you believe this.

Step Five: Believe and Say this Prayer

If you have said the above statement and believe it in your heart, I'd like you to read this prayer out loud, right now. Through this prayer you are telling the Almighty God, Maker of heaven and Earth, that you are serious about what you are going to say. I'd also like you to place your hand over your heart in true confession and humbleness to God as you pray this prayer.

You may want to silently read it first to be sure that you want to enter into this extraordinary new relationship with God.

The Believer's Prayer

Lord Jesus, forgive me for all the wrongs I've done in my life.

I am sorry for all the sinful things I have done against you that hurt both myself and others.

I ask you to clean up my life and bring spiritual health and wealth into my life.

I believe Jesus is the Son of God and that he died on the cross for my sins. And I believe God raised him from the dead by His mighty power.

Right now, Lord Jesus, I invite you into my life and open my heart to you as the Savior and the Lord of all. I receive you into my life and into my heart as my Savior. Amen.

The Word of God, the Bible, says when you say this and really mean it, Jesus comes into your heart and life and gives you a new life of spiritual wealth and richness.

Step Six: Confirm Your Commitment

Let's confirm your commitment today.

You have just prayed to God, and according to that prayer, where is Jesus now?

Answer: He's in your heart and in your life.

And what kind of wealth do you have now?

Answer: Spiritual Wealth in God.

Step Seven: Contact Me about Your New Spiritual Life in Christ.

It's that simple. You now have renewed spiritual life in God through Jesus Christ. I'd like you to contact me so you can grow further in your new-found spiritual life. I will send you some important information about true spiritual wealth in God.

Eternal Life

You also now have what the Bible calls *eternal life*. This means that now and even after you leave this Earth in death, you will be with God and His Son, Jesus Christ, forever. What a tremendous blessing for your future now and later in God's future. That glorious future will include the enjoyment and display of God's wealth. This is, indeed, one of the great joys awaiting the eternal destiny of believers in Christ. The Bible says God will display the variety and magnitude of His wealth during the many phases of the eternal future.

That in the ages to come God might show the incredible wealth of his grace in his kindness toward us through Christ Jesus.

Ephesians 2:7

Please contact me for more information. My information is below.

To grow as a strong believer, you will need to join and be spiritually fed by a good Bible-believing, spiritual church. You must also be connected to strong Christians. If I can help you in this new spiritual walk, please contact me. I'll be sure to get this information to you for free. Now go and live in victory!

Congratulations on Your New Beginning!
May Success and Prosperity Be Yours,

— In the Name of Jesus —

Dr. Kenneth Hammonds

P.O. Box 2853 Inglewood, CA 90305-0853
Email: KH@WealthyThinking.com
Phone: 323-753-1366

A BENEDICTION
Affirming Divine Blessing

A Wealth Benediction

What more fitting close for a wealth commentary than a *Wealth Benediction*? A benediction in its verb form means literally, *to speak good upon* or *to bless*. It is defined as, *to call forth or invoke a blessing from God upon someone or something*. It generally refers to a short blessing. A blessing is, of course, something that benefits or aids in the welfare and prosperity of the one who is blessed. I'm closing with a Wealth Benediction for you. I wish to speak good upon your life and ask God to bless your life with abundance and prosperity. It's from me to you.

I have a twofold purpose for pronouncing this blessing. First, as I have said, this is a blessing *for you*. But second, I wish for you to speak this blessing also *upon others*. The Wealth Benediction is composed of seven verses. There's a wealth blessing for every day of the week.

These little blessings are easily memorized and can be passed on to your children, relatives, and friends. Wouldn't it be great to have your children or grandchildren hearing you pronounce blessings upon them as they go to school everyday? Our children have so much evil and hatred around them; just think of the impact of having someone pronounce blessings upon them.

You can pronounce blessings upon your workplace, business, church, community, your country, or other countries. I earnestly pray a Wealth Benediction for the poorer people and countries of this world, and I expect God to honor my request, especially when I back it up with action.

There are two forms of this benediction. The first is my benediction to you: *A Wealth Benediction for You and for Others.* This is also a bene-diction you can speak into the lives of other people. Following that is the benediction you will pray or speak upon yourself: *A Self-Benediction of Wealth.* Yes, a self-benediction, which is in the form of a self-affirmation. In this self-benediction, the only change is in the personal pronouns; *you, your,* and *yours* are changed to *I, me,* and *mine.* I know you will be tremendously blessed as you speak these out loud to yourself in your devotional time or as you go throughout the day.

A self-benediction is proper. People in the Bible regularly practiced this self-encouraging positive speaking to themselves and to God. David *encouraged himself in the LORD his God.* (1 Samuel 30:6). Jabez, in his now famous prayer, says to God, *Oh, that You would bless me indeed, and enlarge my territory* (1 Chronicles 4:10).

A small group of believers or even an entire nation can call upon God as Israel prayed, *Save now, I pray, O LORD; O LORD, I pray, send now prosperity* (Psalm 118:25). So, you, too, can benefit by changing your self-talk from beating up yourself to a benediction upon yourself.

Thus, as I bless you, I trust you will bless others. How about reading and receiving a blessing a day? A blessing a day will keep stinkin' thinkin' away!

A Wealth Benediction
For You and For Others

From Your Success Coach, Kenneth Hammonds
Seven Verses of Blessings

Verse One
A Benediction for Divine Wealth

*May God's Wealth Surround Your Life Each Day
In Avalanches of Abundance.*

Verse Two
A Benediction for Divine Health and Peace

*May the Grace of His Presence
Bring Health to Your Body and Peace to Your Mind.*

Verse Three
A Benediction for Inner Joy

*May You Enjoy the Wealth of the Universe
as a Visible Expression of God's Majestic Nature.*

Verse Four
A Benediction for Positive Relationships

*May the Abundance of the Almighty Overshadow You
with Rich Relationships and Joyful Expressions of Love.*

Verse Five

A Benediction for Open Doors

May the Wide Door of Opportunity Continually Open before You
that You Might Enter Rich Paths of Purpose and Service.

Verse Six

A Benediction for Showers of Blessings

May God Shower Down upon You from the Windows of Heaven
A Blessing that You Will Not Have Room Enough to Receive.

Verse Seven

A Benediction for God's Revelation

May You Discover the Beauty of
God's Divine Plan as It Unfolds before Your Very Eyes.

May Success, Wealth, and Prosperity be Yours
in Every Area of Your Life.

A Self-Benediction of Wealth

By Your Success Coach, Kenneth Hammonds
Seven Verses of Blessings

Verse One
A Benediction for Divine Wealth

May God's Wealth Surround My Life Each Day
in Avalanches of Abundance.

Verse Two
A Benediction for Divine Health and Peace

May the Grace of His Presence
Bring Health to My Body and Peace to My Mind.

Verse Three
A Benediction for Inner Joy

May I Enjoy the Wealth of the Universe
as a Visible Expression of God's Majestic Nature.

Verse Four
A Benediction for Positive Relationships

May the Abundance of the Almighty Overshadow Me
with Rich Relationships and Joyful Expressions of Love.

Verse Five

A Benediction for Open Doors

May the Wide Door of Opportunity Continually Open before Me
That I Might Enter Rich Paths of Purpose and Service.

Verse Six

A Benediction for Showers of Blessings

May God Shower Down upon Me from the Windows of Heaven
A Blessing that I Will Not Have Room Enough to Receive.

Verse Seven

A Benediction for God's Revelation

May I Discover the Beauty of
God's Divine Plan as It Unfolds before My Very Eyes.

May Success, Wealth, and Prosperity be Mine
in Every Area of My Life.

Appendices

Webster's Seventh New Collegiate Dictionary's Definition:

Appendix: Supplementary material usually attached at the end of a piece of writing.

KH's Definition:

Appendix: After all this writing, I'm still not finished!

The Teacher searched to find just the right words, and what he wrote was upright and true.

And further, my son, be admonished by these. Of making many books there is no end . . .

Ecclesiastes 12:10, 12 (NIV, KJV)

Appendix One

The Bible as the Wealth Book

 A One-Question Quiz

Name the book that's worth more than its weight in gold.

The Answer:

Your law is more valuable to me than millions [of dollars] in gold and silver!

Psalm 119:72 (NLT)

In Chapter 2, I boldly declared the Bible as a Wealth Book. I'd like to expand that idea here.

The Price of the Gutenberg Bible

Johannes Gutenberg invented the movable type printing press. The first book he printed in 1456 was the Latin Bible. So, the Bible is the first book ever printed. On October 22, 1987, a company in Japan bought one of the Gutenberg Bibles at an auction for a staggering 4.9 million dollars! So, the Bible really is worth millions of dollars. If the book itself is worth 4.9 million dollars, how much are its **contents** worth to you? Have you entrusted your spiritual and financial future to its wealthy wisdom?

The Bestselling Wealth Book Ever

One book has been on the bestseller list throughout all human eras and in all cultures. This bestseller is available in bookstores all over the globe and translated into hundreds of languages. It tells us about creating and preserving wealth. It's a book about debt reduction and full of ideas and motivational hints about ensuring a wealthy future for you and your family.

This book features more than forty famous writers and recounts the highs and lows of many millionaires and billionaires of ancient history. And one billionaire has written extensively about obtaining and maintaining money, success, wealth, and fortune. It is available for a reasonable price at your local bookstore and in some places your may get it, or portions of it, for no cost at all.

What is this book? It's THE Book, the Bible—the Ancient Wealth Book. One of the reasons for the Wealth Book is so poverty in all its forms can be eradicated from the Earth and from human experience.

This book is a Message from God to humans about how to live a life of abundance and joy. Yes, God wants you to produce and enjoy wealth in every area of your life. It's NOT just a material wealth thing—it's a full wealth experience.

Some of Its Wealth-Building Principles

The wisdom of this advice in Proverbs 14:23 (NIV) is simple, yet profound:

All hard work brings a profit,
but mere talk leads only to poverty.

Or, how about a clear truism like Proverbs 10:4 (NIV)?

Lazy hands make a man poor,
but diligent hands bring wealth.

Or, how about Jesus' famous statement balancing true wealth in Mark 8:36 (NKJV)?

> *For what will it profit a man if he gains*
> *the whole world, and loses his own soul?*

The Greek word for "soul" here in Mark 8:36 is *psychē*, which also means *life* or *mind*. And it's a probing question using any of the meanings of *psychē* in the translation. What profit could there possibly be for a person to gain all the wealth of the world and to lose his or her mind, life, or soul in the process? A dead millionaire or crazy billionaire has only made his or her riches for others to squander after the committal.

Or, let's get inspired by the great declaration of financial independence of Deuteronomy 8:18.

But remember the LORD your God, for it is he who gives you the ability to produce wealth, and so confirms his covenant, which he swore to your forefathers, as it is today.

You'll need wealthy tour guides and guidelines to live a wealthy life. The Wealth Book is full of time-tested wealth-building principles. Some of the richest men and women spiritually and materially who ever lived are mentioned in the Bible. The wisdom of the ages and experiences of the rich and wise (the good, the bad, and the ugly) have been generously passed on to us.

The Bible Speaks Extensively Concerning Wealth

The Bible speaks much about wealth, since wealth is a vital part of the human experience. The KJV has over 1,100 references to wealth or wealthy, or expensive materials (wealth, rich[es], gold, silver, jewel[ry], money, precious stones, and the spoils of war, not counting the many references to expensive clothing, fragrances, spices, oils, etc.) The wisdom of the written Word is more valuable than material wealth because it is an exceedingly precious gift from God and because it brings full wealth to all who follow its principles. It is a wealth book "worth its weight in gold," and then some. If you love good books, you'll love this one!

If you like Bible statistics, maybe you'd like to know that the word *God* in the KJV occurs 3,091 times. The word *man* (or *men*) occurs 3,012 times. And the words for wealth and expensive materials mentioned above occur 1,106 times. So, I suppose we can say the Bible is a book about God, man, and wealth. The ancient poet and hymn writer has expounded so eloquently regarding the value of this Wealth Book to humanity:

Your law is more valuable to me than millions in gold and silver!
Psalm 119:72 (NLT)

Because I love your commands more than gold, more than pure gold, ...
Psalm 119:127 (NIV)

Yes, there are many other good books on wealth acquisition, utilization, and distribution. But, all these great books are but a pale canvas compared to the beautiful portrait of wealthy existence painted by the Author of human wealth. Because, in order to have an accurate picture of true wealth, all these other wealth books must adhere to the high righteous standards and time proven system of THE Wealth Book.

Appendix Two

Biblical Hebrew Words for Wealth

Facility in the biblical languages has long been recognized as a basic requirement for pastoral ministry. No person is likely to grasp the intended meaning of the Bible, on its deepest level, unless that person learns to read and, in some sense, think in [or at least understand word studies in] Hebrew and Greek.

David Alan Black,
Using New Testament Greek in Ministry

This Appendix is, of course, not intended to make an individual a Hebrew scholar. However, some knowledge of Hebrew words for wealth will shed light upon our study of the meaning of wealth in the Bible. I hope these insights will inspire you toward further study.

The many biblical Hebrew words for *wealth* and *abundance* are translated differently by the English versions of the Bible, depending upon the context. It is not my purpose to enter into all the subtle meanings of Hebrew words. I simply wish to show how Bible translations are liberal in giving the Hebrew words different English usages. I will focus on five OT Hebrew words: *Sharats, Chayil, Koach, Hown,* and *Tov.* The word *Shalom* (peace, prosperity, wholeness, health) has already been discussed in Chapter 5 in the section on the "P" of the P.I.E.S. Wealthy Cycle.

213

1. Sharats (pronounced shar-RATS)

Sometimes the KJV translates the Hebrew word *sharats* as "great" or "rich." The NIV translates it as "wealthy." *Sharats* literally means to swarm or abound. It also indicates breeding (bringing forth, increasing) in abundance.

Scriptures (KJV and NIV translations)

- Genesis 1:20. KJV: *bring forth abundantly*, NIV: *teem with*
- Genesis 8:17. KJV: *breed abundantly*, NIV: *can multiply*
- Genesis 13:2. KJV: *Abram was very rich*, NIV: *Abram had become very wealthy*
- 2 Samuel 19:32. KJV: **Barzillai . . . was a very great man.* NIV: *Barsillai. . .was a very wealthy man.*

2. Chayil (Pronounced KA-yeal)

Chayil and *sharats* are the primary Hebrew words translated as "wealth" in the OT. The basic meaning of *chayil* in the Hebrew OT is strength, power, a force, or an army. *Chayil* speaks of ability. The point here is: wealth brings power to one's life. Wealth brings with it the ability to perform.

Scriptures (KJV and NIV Translations)

- Numbers 31:14. KJV, NIV: *battle*
- Genesis 34:29. KJV, NIV: *wealth*
- Deuteronomy 8:17-18. KJV, NIV: *wealth*
- Joshua 1:14. KJV: men *of valour*, NIV: *fully armed*

Chayil also means *riches*. "Rich" is a nice word and a nice thing to be. For when you are rich in anything, you have enough to give to others.

The English word "rich" also has as its root, meaning *powerful*. To be

---

* Barzillai was a wealthy supporter of King David. Leaders need wealthy support to finance their campaigns, building projects, business enterprises, and their political, spiritual, and social programs. Do you have wealthy supporters and/or mentors for your vision? If not, why not?

rich means to be abounding in natural resources, to be extremely productive. The quality of richness is, of course, not only material; at its core,
it is spiritual and relational. For only God is naturally omni-abundant in
His nature and attributes and omni-prolific in His works. His vast created universe makes this clearly observable.

3. Koach (Pronounced KO-ack)

The basic meaning of the word *koach* is similar to the meaning of *chayil*. It also means *strength or might*, and is translated by many English
words. It's only translated "wealth" once in the KJV. In Proverbs 5:10: *Lest
strangers be filled with thy wealth; and thy labours be in the house of a
stranger.* It is in a complicated context but seems to be used here to indicate the strength and vigor of the physical body (health) in which illicit
sexual relations with an adulteress (female) sucks the life's blood and
physical strength of the adulterer (male). (In the context verse, 11
[NRSV] adds, *And at the end of your life you will groan, when your flesh
and body are consumed.* The NLT vividly reads: *Afterward you will groan
in anguish when disease consumes your body.*)

It may be difficult at first to see how the Bible translators could translate this Hebrew word, *koach*, into the English word "wealth." But, if we
understand the main idea of wealth to be the power or strength to do
what you desire, then the explanation is clearer. So, health is strength or
wealth in the body.

Scriptures (KJV and NIV translations)

+ Genesis 4:12. KJV: yield unto thee her *strength*, NIV: yield its *crops*
+ Deuteronomy 8:18. KJV: *power to* get wealth, NIV: *ability* to produce
+ Proverbs 5:10. KJV: NIV: *wealth*
+ Job 6:22. KJV: of your *substance*, NIV: from your *wealth*

4. Hown (Pronounced HONE)

The Hebrew word, *hown*, means wealth, enough, or sufficiency. It refers
to that which is plenteous and something that is high in value or price.

It refers to that which is or those who are affluent and rich. In the KJV, this word is sometimes translated as *substance*. It appears mostly in the Book of Proverbs.

Scriptures (KJV and NIV translations)

+ Psalm 112:3. KJV, NIV: *Wealth* and riches shall be (NIV:are) in his house (said of the individual who fears the Lord and delights in his commandments).
+ Proverbs 3:9. KJV: Honour the LORD with thy *substance*, NIV: with your *wealth*
+ Proverbs 10:15. KJV: The rich man's *wealth* is his strong city, NIV: The *wealth* of the rich
+ Proverbs 29:3. KJV: but he that keepeth company with harlots spendeth his *substance*, NIV: but a companion of prostitutes squanders his *wealth*
+ Song of Songs 8:7. I think we need to look at the entire verse in the Bible's *Love Songbook*. It shows wealth does have its limits! I have placed the verse in its Hebrew poetry triadic form (three lines). It seems to read with much more clarity and emotion this way.

KJV
Line 1: *Many waters cannot quench love, neither can the floods drown it:*
Line 2: *if a man would give all the substance of his house for love,*
Line 3: *it would utterly be contemned.*

NIV
Many waters cannot quench love; rivers cannot wash it away.
If one were to give all the wealth of his house for love,
it would be utterly scorned.

This means when a human loves deeply and truly, neither the strength of powerful oceans, nor the currents of mighty rivers can extinguish the flame of love. Indeed, this lover-poet brazenly states, *Love is as strong as death.* Verse six, which is the background for verse seven, is quoted in full below, again in its Hebrew poetry triadic form.

NIV
Place me like a seal over your heart, like a seal on your arm;
for love is as strong as death, its jealousy unyielding as the grave.
It burns like blazing fire, like a mighty flame.

The lover now in verse seven moves to a great crescendo at the ending of this passionate love song. He states that all the net worth of a rich man cannot extinguish the strong love of a man or a woman. My! My! I wonder if that kind of love exists today?

5. Tōv (Pronounced tōv, like the "o" in stove.)
Some Bible students may recognize *tov* as the Hebrew word for "good." This is the word used in Genesis when God looked at His creation and said, "It (this beautiful new creation) is good (*tov*)."

Tov has the idea of physical or moral goodness or excellence in quality. In the Genesis creation passage, *tov* is probably best translated as, "It is excellent!" One can only imagine the pristine beauty and excellence of a newly created universe as it comes directly from the hand of Almighty God.

Brown Driver and Briggs (BDB), the premier Biblical Hebrew Lexicon, defines *tov* primarily as good, pleasing, sweet, and agreeable to the senses. It goes on to define it as meaning *prosperous, valuable, precious, happiness, benefit, or simply, good things.*

Here are some Bible verses using the Hebrew word *tov.*

In the day of prosperity[tov]be joyful, but in the day of adversity consider: God also hath set the one over against the other, to the end that man should find nothing after him.

Ecclesiastes 7:14 (KJV)

I say to the LORD, "You are my Lord; I have no good [tov/ prosperity] apart from you."

Psalm 16:2 (NRSV)

BDB translates the phrase, *is not my welfare [prosperity] dependent upon thee?*

"Submit to God and be at peace with him; in this way prosperity[tov] will come to you.

Job 22:21 (NIV)

You crown the year with Your goodness [tov/prosperity], and Your paths drip with abundance.

Psalm 65:11 (NKJV)

Who is the man that fears the LORD? Him shall He teach in the way He chooses. He himself shall dwell in prosperity[tov], and his descendants shall inherit the earth.

Psalm 25:12–13 (NKJV)

Who fed you in the wilderness with manna, which your fathers did not know, that He might humble you and that He might test you, to do you good [tov/prosper you] in the end. . . .

Deuteronomy 8:16 (NKJV)

Mordecai, one of the great ancient leaders of Israel, knew that *tov* was essential for people. When he saw the spiritual, economic, and political plight of Israel, he began *seeking the wealth [tov] of his people.* (Esther 10:3, KJV)

The noun and verb forms of *tov* appear in the OT 590 times. The NT words for good (kalos and agathos) appear 243 times. So, all totaled, the word "good" appears 944 times in the Bible.

Without a doubt, the Bible is the *Good Book*, the Prosperity Book.

This description of wealth reminds us that wealth is good and can be utilized to produce much good. Wealth also helps promote excellence and quality (Job 21:13). Everything from quality healthcare to quality schools and quality housing can only come about when there is wealth. Now that's good doing GOOD!

A Summary of the OT Hebrew Words for Wealth

1. Sharats (Pronounced shar-RATS) = Abounding

Wealth means having plenty, abounding in resources.
Wealthy living is therefore: **an abundant life**.

2. Chayil (Pronounced KA-yeal) = Power

Wealth means having power in one's life.
Wealthy living is therefore: **a powerful life**, or empowered living. It's asserting power over one's self and one's circumstances. It's being fully armed for the battles of life.

3. Koach (Pronounced KO-ack) = Strength in Body, Health

Wealth means having strength and health. (wealth in the body)
Wealthy living is therefore: **a healthy life**.

4. Hown (Pronounced HONE, like phone) = Plenty (of something valuable)

Wealth means having plenty of something valuable.
Wealthy living is therefore: **a plenteous life**.

5. Tov (Pronounced tōv, like the "o" in stove) = Good, Excellent, Prosperity, Happiness

Wealth means having that which is good morally or physically, excellent in quality, pleasing, and sweet. It means happiness, prosperity, or simply, having good things or – the GOOD LIFE.
Wealthy living is therefore: **a happy, prosperous, good life**.

Biblical Words for Wealth: Conclusion

So, in the English translations of the Hebrew concepts of wealth, there are ideas of great, abundant, plenteous, and valuable. Wealth is power and strength and gives humans the ability to do and perform great things. Wealth also means health in the body. And finally, wealth means excellence of quality and prosperity. Wealth in any area of your life is good. It is not evil. It is certainly good to have the ability to do good. So, in the OT, the word wealth is used for the material, spiritual, and physical dimensions of life.

A full study of all of the words used for abundance and wealth in the Bible would take a very large volume. For then, the study must include words like: great, large, cattle, sheep, oxen, land, gold, silver, rich, and so on. I hope this will be the subject of another volume or another author! These five Hebrew words and the many biblical possessions and materials for wealth confirm the Bible again as a Book of Wealth and our God as the God of Wealth and Abundance.

Appendix Three

Releasing the Wealth Builder in Children

A KH Quotable Quote

*Teach children first how to handle themselves,
then it will be easier to teach them how to handle their money.*

Teaching the principles of wealth building and God's Wealth Cycle, P.I.E.S. (Producing, Increasing, Enjoying, and Sharing wealth), to children will have a dramatic, positive influence on them for the rest of their lives. Here are some practical ways to begin to teach these principles to your children, nieces, nephews, and grandchildren.

A Few Beginning Ideas

+ Let children know they can do anything they put their minds to do, and they CAN produce wealth.
+ Get children involved in the family business, if there is one. If there's not a family business, have them start their own in a small way.
+ Let them work at home, in school, and elsewhere.
+ If you are well off financially, don't let your children know or think they have got it made financially. They still need to respect the labor and toil that's involved in getting money. After all, "Money doesn't grow on trees."

✦ Teach them of the perils and pain of debt, especially credit card debt. I remember the excitement on my older daughter's face when I got her her first credit card as a teenager. She was on *cloud nine.* However, when she found out it was an American Express Card, and it needed to be paid off each month, she was brought back to Earth in a flash! However, I did have a purpose: to train her in proper credit card usage. Since that time, she regularly pays off all her bills in thirty days. One large, five-year financial obligation was paid off in one year. My advice is: don't get a Visa for your teenager unless you carefully watch the card charges. No matter what card they receive, or if they have none at all, teach them the pains and perils of debt.

Special Note to Single Mothers with Sons

Mothers, please insist that your sons take care of themselves: they should make their own beds, learn how to cook, do their chores around the house, and start doing some little things to make money with the talents they have. Don't raise them with the mentality that, "I don't need to do anything because Mama (or some other woman) will always take care of me." Let them know they need to take care of themselves and then take care of others. Remind them that you, as the mother, are on Earth to assist them in learning this lesson in personal accountability. They will gain greater responsibility and be an asset rather than a burden to you later in life.

So, does your teenage son say he's "got to have" a pair of those $200.00 designer tennis shoes? (Any son younger than that certainly does NOT need those shoes!) No problem. Have your teenage son find and do odd jobs to earn this money for these "must have" shoes.

The Book of Proverbs has much beneficial advise for raising sound, godly children. One of its most outstanding statements says,

Train up a child in the way he should go: and when he is old, he will not depart from it.

Proverbs 22:6 (KJV)

The KH Child Raising Financial Paraphrase of Proverbs 22:6

Train up a child in the financially responsible way he should go, and when he is old he won't keep coming back to you for a loan!

Hints Regarding When to Teach the Wealth Cycle

One of the best ways to teach anything to children is to model it and make it a natural part of everyday life for you and for them. Teach them in the little educational moments that arise during the course of a day and start at an early age. It's never too early to start your child on the way toward financial responsibility and wealth. Also, there are some great children's books on money. Go to the local library or bookstore and find one appropriate for your child's level.

However, remember YOU are your child's greatest book because you are the *living book* read continually by your children. And your financial behavior, good or bad, is also read by others and placed in a credit report. (Space prohibits me from delivering my impassioned dissertation on the importance of good credit for the believer in Christ. This is just a reminder note to stir you up.)

It is said, (a KH adaptation of an anonymous saying) "*Our children's ears are sometimes closed to our advice, but their eyes are ever open to our example.*"

Assist your children in living out God's Wealth Cycle in their lives, and you'll give them a gift more precious than money. For the lessons of wealth are more valuable than the possession of money.

Houses and wealth [material goods and financial wisdom] are inherited from parents.

Proverbs 19:14 (NIV)

Appendix Four

The Wealth Continuum: Six Abundance/Financial Levels in the Movement from Poverty to Wealth

⌒ A KH Question ⌒

*Where are YOU among the six levels
in the movement from poverty to wealth?*

In this appendix, I'd like to give more detail to my Wealth Continuum mentioned in Chapter 3. The Wealth Continuum is a series of six abundance/financial levels from poverty to wealth. Below is a visual representation.

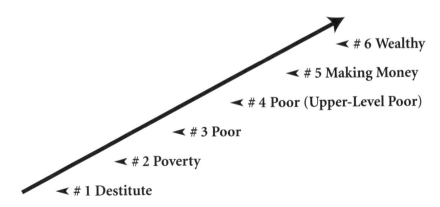

◄ # 6 Wealthy

◄ # 5 Making Money

◄ # 4 Poor (Upper-Level Poor)

◄ # 3 Poor

◄ # 2 Poverty

◄ # 1 Destitute

LEVEL # 1: Destitute (Example: The Woman of 2 Kings Chapter 4)

Description: Extreme poverty and no assistance, sometimes also including some form of extreme debt. This is a barren existence because there are few, if any, outside resources providing help (No significant government or social assistance exists.) Some have termed this *abject* poverty.

Personal Productivity: No personally produced income or utilization of inner resources and skills.

LEVEL # 2: Poverty

Description: Not making it with one's own resources; totally dependent on outside resources for one's existence; living off handouts. (*Some* government or social assistance exists.)

Personal Productivity: No personally produced income or utilization of inner resources and skills.

LEVEL # 3: Poor (Broke)

Description: Just enough to get by. Just making ends meet. There is NO extra. These are the working poor.

Personal Productivity: Little is made from one's own resources.

LEVEL # 4: Poor 2 (Upper-Level Poor)

Description: Making some money, but in debt. The bottom line is minus rather than plus.

Personal Productivity: Making money from one's own skills, experience, or job. Unfortunately, these individuals only utilize minimum usage of their inner resources and skills. And because of that, they usually also make minimum or lower wages.

LEVEL # 5: Making Money

Description: There is enough money, but there are NO significant savings or financial investments.

Personal Productivity: Unlike Level #4 above, these individuals are making plenty of money. They make more than the average wage earner but have not utilized the greater potential within to produce higher levels of prosperity.

LEVEL # 6: Wealthy

Description: At this level, there is money *plus* investments and abundant material resources. However, experiencing *true* wealth at this level also includes an abundant quality of life, liberty, and love. True wealth experiences this abundance in each of the ten dimensions of life (spiritual, intellectual, emotional, material, financial, physical, social, occupational, environmental, and time). Many sub-levels exists within the wealthy level. And each level of an individual's wealth experience is to increase, improve, and go higher.

Some persons at this wealthy level may be high in material wealth but low in relationship wealth. The challenge for these individuals is to develop their important personal relationships and experience a wealth of satisfaction in this area of their lives, also. The challenge for the wealthy is to spread the wealth throughout their personal lives at the same level it is experienced in their occupational and material dimensions.

Personal Productivity: Unlike those at levels 1 through 5 above, these individuals are experts at creating wealth and abundance in society. They, therefore, reap the benefits of their creativity, business efforts, and entrepreneurial savvy. They don't necessarily possess greater inner raw skill or talent, but they do possess to a greater degree the passionate commitment to becoming financially free and are persistent in the attainment of their dreams.

Observe the global human society and you will notice not only individuals, but families, groups, communities, businesses, and nations will also be positioned somewhere on the six levels of the Wealth Continuum.

Wealthy Resources

A Bibliography for Wealth Builders

In this wealthy bibliography, you will discover financial books and resources to further advance your study of wealth.

+ Financial Resources: General Information for the Investor
+ More Financial Resources: Reading Financial Newspapers
+ Financial Resources for Women
+ Social and Historical Perspectives on Wealth and Poverty
+ Developing Home Based Businesses, Other Money Making Ideas
+ Some of the Biblical Resources Used in this Study
+ Biblical/Theological Wealth Resources
+ Ethnic Groups and Wealthy Thinking (African American, African, Jewish, Latino)
+ General Inspirational Ideas and Motivation
+ Success Devotional Readings
+ Professional Growth

Wealthy Resources

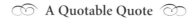

A Quotable Quote

Of making many books there is no end.
Ecclesiastes 12:12 (KJV)

1. Financial Resources:
General Information for the Investor

Books

Millionaires in Training, by George B. Thompson, Prosperity
Publishing, 1999.
(Mr. Thompson is the originator of a program called Millionaires in
Training (MIT). The MIT program has been a part of my School of
Success (SOS) for a number of years. The MIT training focuses on
understanding money and financial instruments. His particular
focus is on the stock market. It is an excellent beginning guide to
wealth building. It's superb. Get it! The Web site is www.trainingmil-
lionaires.com.)
*The Motley Fool Investment Guide: How the Fools Beat Wall Street's Wise
Men and How You Can Too,* David and Tom Gardner, Simon &
Schuster, 1996.
Sound Mind Investing, Austin Pryor, Moody Press, 1996.
*Investments that Fit You: How to Develop a Strategy Based on Your
Personality Type (Sound Mind Investing Strategies),* Austin Pryor,
Moody Press, 1995.
10 Minute Guide to Working with Financial Advisors, Barbara Hetzer,
Macmillan Spectrum/Alpha Books, 1997.
Wealth in a Decade, Brett Machtig, Irwin Professional Publishing, 1997.
Official Netscape Guide to Online Investments, Russell Shaw, Ventana
Communications Group, 1996.
*It's About the Money: The Fourth Movement of the Freedom Symphony:
How to Build Wealth, Get Access to Capital, and Achieve Your
Financial Dreams,* Jesse, Sr. Jackson, Jesse L., Jr. Jackson, et al, Times
Books, 2000.

A Significant Newspaper and Magazine

Investor Business Daily (IBD)
I like IBD. It's written in plain English and helps the beginner to understand the financial terms and times. It particularly serves those seeking to understand investing in the stock market, and as a plus, it has an excellent section called Leaders & Success. Each day, it highlights various leaders and principles of successful people.

Money Magazine
This has been an excellent magazine for everyday people for a number of years. It always has a number of articles in every area of major concern in money management and finances.

The Internet

"The Net" has numerous Web sites for the beginners and experts. The free access to financial information gives valuable help for anyone willing to research it. If you are not familiar with the Internet or Internet resources, get busy today and start learning about what is available. Web sites, Yahoo, Microsoft, CNN, and Morning Star are particularly valuable for information and for keeping up with your investments. Of course, there are numerous Web sites for the many financial institutions and industries— real estate, computer technology, etc. If it is a human endeavor, it is on the Internet. You can use this resource to become more knowledgeable about money for little or no cost. Even if you don't have a computer, you can go to the library or a school and "surf" the Net. You are without excuse. You must study money if you expect to preserve and increase the value of the money you have worked so hard to earn.

2. More Financial Resources: reading financial newspapers

Reading Financial Newspapers, Peter Passell, Warner Books, 1986.
Investing Smart: How to Pick Winning Stocks with Investor's Business Daily, Dhun H, Sethna, McGraw-Hill, 1997.
The Wall Street Journal: The Dow Jones-Irwin Guide to Using, Michael B. Lehmann, Dow Jones-Irwin, 1984.

3. Financial Resources for Women

The Women's Guide to the Stock Market, Barbara Lee, Ballantine Books, 1982.
Money Doesn't Grow on Trees: A Parent's Guide to Raising Financially Responsible Children, Neale S. Godfrey and Carolina Edwards, Simon & Schuster, 1994.
The Financially Confident Woman, Mary Hunt, Broadman & Holman Publishers, 1996.
The Family Manager, Kathy Peel, Word Publishing, 1996.

4. Social and Historical Perspectives on Wealth and Poverty

Sharing the Wealth: Workers and the World Economy, Ethan B. Kapstein, W.W. Norton & Company, 1999.
The Wealth and Poverty of Nations: Why Some Are So Rich and Some So Poor, David S. Landes, W.W. Norton & Company, 1999.
The Wealth of Cities: Revitalizing the Centers of American Life, John O. Norquist, Perseus Press, 1999.
The War on the Poor: A Defense Manual, Randy Albelda, Nancy Folbre, and the Center for Popular Economics, The New York Press, 1996.

5. Developing Home-Based Businesses, Other Money Making Ideas

The One Minute Millionaire: The Enlightened Way To Wealth, Mark Victor Hansen and Robert G. Allen, Harmony Books, 2002.
Multiple Streams of Income: How to Generate a Lifetime of Unlimited Wealth, Robert G. Allen, John Wiley & Sons, 2000.
Multiple Streams of Internet Income: How Ordinary People Make Extraordinary Money Online, Robert G. Allen, John Wiley & Sons, 2001.
How to Make Millions with Your Ideas: An Entrepreneur's Guide, Dan S. Kennedy, Plume Books, 1996.
Honey, I Want to Start My Own Business: A Planning Guide for Couples, Azriela Jaffe, Harper Business, 1996.
Turn Your Ideas into Money, Jeff Spira, Chilton Book Company, 1990.

Speak and Grow Rich, Dottie & Lilly Walters, Prentice Hall, 1989.
199 Great Home Businesses You Can Start (and Succeed In) for Under $1,000: How to Choose the Best Home Business for You Based on Your Personality Type, Tyler G. Hicks, Prima Publishing, 1999.
The 150 Most Profitable Home Businesses for Women, Katrina Z. Jones, Adams Media Corporation, 2000.
Success for Less: 100 Low-Cost Businesses You Can Start Today, Rob and Terry Adams, Entrepreneur Media, Inc., 1999.
Wealth Starts at Home: 15 Secrets That Could Make You a Fortune, David D'Arcangelo, Irwin Professional Publishing, 1997.
The Home Business and Small Business Answer Book: Solutions to the Most Frequently Asked Questions about Starting and Running Your Business, (2nd edition) by Janet Attard, Henry Holt & Company, 2000.
Work At Home Moms, a Web site: WAHM.com. This is a great Web resource, and there is a book too, entitled, *The Work-at-Home Mom's Guide to Home Business: Stay at Home and Make Money with WAHM.com,* by Cheryl Demos, Hazen Publishers, 2000.

6. Some of the Biblical Resources Used in This Study

The IVP Bible Background Commentary: New Testament, by Craig Keener. Intervarsity Press, 1993.
(Dr. Keener is a great scholar, and this is a unique commentary. It highlights the historical customs and background of Roman, Greek, and Jewish history.)
Linguistic Key to the Greek New Testament, Fritz Rienecker and Cleon Rogers. Zondervan, 1980.
(This commentary is best utilized by those who know NT Greek and Greek grammar. However, this great Biblical resource may also be useful for diligent students of the NT.)
Theological Dictionary of the New Testament, edited by Gerhard Kittel and Gerhard Friedrich. William B. Eerdmans, 1985.
The Holy Scriptures of the Old Testament Hebrew and English, The British & Foreign Bible Society, 1970.
The Englishman's Hebrew and Chaldee Concordance of the Old Testament, 5th edition, Zondervan, 1970.

An Intermediate Greek-English Lexicon: Founded upon the Seventh Edition of Liddell and Scott's Greek-English Lexicon, Oxford Press, 1986.

A Greek-English Lexicon of the New Testament and Other Early Christian Literature (Walter Bauer) by William F. Arndt and F. Wilbur Gingrich. 2nd Edition, The University of Chicago Press, 1979.

The New Greek-English Interlinear New Testament (United Bible Societies' Fourth Corrected Edition, Same text as *Novum Testamentum Graece,* 26th edition) Tyndale House Publishers, 1990.

Spirit Filled Life Bible, New King James Version, General Editor, Jack W. Hayford, Thomas Nelson Publishers, 1991.

The NIV Study Bible, New International Version, General Editor, Kenneth Barker, Zondervan Bible Publishers, 1985.

A Hebrew and English Lexicon of the Old Testament, with an Appendix Containing the Biblical Aramaic, based on the Lexicon of William Gesenius, by Francis Brown, S.R. Driver, and Charles A. Briggs. Oxford, 1968.

Quick Verse Version 4.0e CD ROM, Parsons Technology, 1992–1996 (With Strong's Bible Dictionary, and five translations: King James Version, New King James Version, New International Version, New Revised Standard Version, and New Living Translation.)

7. Biblical/Theological Wealth Resources

Theo-economics, Dr. Roland Hill.
(This is an excellent Christian view of economics, hence the tile Theo-economics. Dr. Hill offers insightful information and analysis of God's command in the economic structures of society. Available from the Freedom Foundation, Inc. P.O. Box 133 Keene, TX 76059 817-645-3258)

Escape from Debtors Prison: Got Money? Rachelle & Tyrone Potts, El Shaddai Publishing, 2000.

The Wealth of the World: The Proven Transfer System, John Avanzini, Harrison House, 1989.
(A number of titles come from this Christian financial expert. His Web site, www.avanzini.org, is loaded with a wealth of information

regarding the Christian and finances. You can also check any
Christian bookstore for titles by him.)

Wealth as Peril and Obligation: The New Testament on Possessions,
Sondra Ely Wheeler, William B. Eerdmans, 1995.

Foolproof Finances: Financial Survival from the Bible, David Mallonee,
Kingdom, 1995.

*Thinking Theologically about Faith and Wealth: A Seven Session Study
Guide,* Dr. Carol Johnston.
(This research paper is available from The Christian Theological
Seminary Web site, cts.edu/FACULTY/johnston/wealth.html. CTS is
in Indianapolis, Indiana.)

Thinking Theologically About Wealth Including Money, Dr. Carol
Johnston.
(This research paper is available from The Christian Theological
Seminary Web site, cts.edu/FACULTY/johnston/wealth.html. CTS is
in Indianapolis, Indiana.)

8. Ethnic Groups and Wealthy Thinking (African American, African, Jewish, Latino)

The resources in this section show that the wealth cycle can work in any
culture, country, or continent. When it is ignored, there is poverty and
ruin for individuals, groups, and nations.

African American

Think and Grow Rich: A Black Choice, Dennis Kimbro and Napoleon Hill,
Fawcett Colombine, 1991.

Black Wealth: Your Road to Small Business Success, Robert L. Wallace, John
Wiley & Sons, 2000.

Black Entrepreneurs in America: Stories of Struggle and Success, Michael D.
Woodard, Rutgers University Press, 1997.

*Wealth Building Lessons of Booker T. Washington – For a New Black
America,* T. M. Pryor, Duncan & Duncan, 1995.

*How to Succeed in Business Without Being White: Straight Talk on Making
it in America,* Earl G. Graves, Harper Business, 1997.

"Why Should White Guys Have All the Fun?": How Reginald Lewis Created a Billion-Dollar Business Empire, Reginald F. Lewis and Blair S. Walker, John Wiley & Sons, 1995.

Africa: General

Africa's Economic Hope in the Middle of Despair, The Central Bank of
   Kenya. (An e-book at Web site: www.centralbank.go.ke/cbk/Africa
   Hope.)
   Below is the statement from the Introduction:
   *The contents of this booklet are based on presentation material and
   a speech made by Micah Cheserem, Governor of the Central Bank of
   Kenya on 13th March, 1998 during the closing of the Domestic Debt
   Management Workshop organized by the Commonwealth Secretariat
   at the Kenya School of Monetary Studies. The Workshop was attended
   by participants from fifteen African countries.*
   The theme of both the presentation and the speech is economic
   hope for those African countries implementing appropriate market-
   driven economic reforms. I would add that there is hope only if the
   P.I.E.S wealth cycle is implemented sincerely and vigorously.

Africa: Nigeria

Wealth of the Yoruba People, Kayode J. Fakinlede, Morris Publishing, 2000.

Africa: Kenya

*Our Solution Our Problems: An Economic and Public Policy Agenda for
   Kenya*, A Publication Compiled By The Institute of Economic
   Affairs, Edited by Wamuyu Gatheru and Robert Shaw, 1998. (An e-
   book at Web site: www.iea.or.ke)

Jewish

The Jewish Phenomenon: Seven Keys to the Enduring Wealth of a People,
   Steven Silbiger, Longstreet Press, 2000.
   (Silbiger has some great appendices and end notes that mention
   several resources for more study of Jewish life, thought, culture,
   and history. I highly recommend this book to the reader for its
   information and as a source for finding other resources for study.)

Chutzpah, Alan Dershowitz, Simon & Shuster, 1991.
The Complete Idiot's Guide to Jewish History and Culture, Rabbi Benjamin Blech, Alpha Books, 1999.

Latino

The Americano Dream: How Latinos Can Achieve Success in Business and in Life, Lionel Sosa, Plume, 1999.
The Latino Guide to Personal Money Management, Laura Castaneda, Laura Castellanos, Bloomberg Press, 1999.
Yes You Can! Si!, Se Puede: Every Latino's Guide to Building Family Wealth, Charles Gonzalez, Chandler House Press, 1998.

9. General Inspirational Ideas and Motivation

The Million Dollar Secret Hidden in Your Mind, Anthony Novell, Harper & Row Publishers, 1973.
How to Be Rich, J. Paul Getty, A Jove Book, 1965.
Your Infinite Power to Be Rich, Joseph Murphy, Parker Publishing, 1966.
Think & Grow Rich Action Pack, Napoleon Hill, A Plumb Book, 1990.
Acres of Diamonds, Russell H. Conwell, Jove Books, 1988.
Rags to Riches: Motivating Stories of How Ordinary People Achieved Extraordinary Wealth!, Gail Liberman and Alan Lavine, Dearborn, 2000.
The Instant Millionaire: A Tale of Wisdom and Wealth, Mark Fisher, New World Library, 1990.
The Millionaire Next Door, Thomas J. Stanley and William D. Danko, Longstreet Press, 1996.
(This bestselling book enlightens us as to the real lifestyles of America's millionaires. This is a must read for those who think of millionaires as high-flying spenders. By the way, what's the big deal about the millionaire status? There are over 5 million millionaires in the United States.)
How to Think Like a Millionaire, Mark Fisher with Marc Allen, New World Library, 1997.

10. Success Devotional Readings

God's Little Devotional Book on Success, compiled by W. B. Freeman Concepts, Inc., Honor Books Inc., 1997.

Winning 101 Devotional, Van Crouch, Honor Books, Inc., 1998.

From Faith to Faith: A Daily Guide to Victory, Kenneth and Gloria Copeland, Kenneth Copeland Pub., 1996.

11. Professional Growth

How to Be the Person Successful Companies Fight to Keep: The Insider's Guide to Being Number One in the Workplace, Connie Podesta and Jean Gatz, Simon & Schuster, 1997.

Multipreneuring, Tom Gorman, Simon & Schuster, 1996.

Beat the Odds: Career Buoyancy Tactics for Today's Turbulent Job Market, Martin Yate, Ballantine Books, 1995.

Closing

Webster's Seventh New Collegiate Dictionary's Definition:

Closing: To come to an end or period.

KH's Definition:

Closing: After all this writing, I'm finally finished!
(until the next book)

I have brought you glory on earth by completing the work you gave me to do.

Jesus Christ, John 17:4, NIV

Epilogue

My Vision for Wealth

 A KH Quotable Quote

I see wealth for all and in all. What do you see?

The writing of *God Wants You to be Wealthy: How to Release the Wealth Builder Within* has issued forth from my vision of the world as God originally designed it—opulent and wealthy in everyway.

My Vision is to see God's people enjoying the wealth for which they were created.

My Mission is to encourage people to embrace the compatibility of spirituality and wealth — properly linking them and bringing them into spiritual harmony in their lives.

It Is Also My Mission to coach and inspire individuals, communities, and nations to release the wealth builder within.

In my vision, I see God's wealth and prosperity flowing throughout the streets of every country, city, and community; for every man, woman, and child; to every race, size, and color of humanity; in every social, economic, and political situation. *I see wealth for all and in all.* What do *you* see?

For me, the message (vision and mission) of *God Wants You to be Wealthy* is not merely an academic exercise reserved for the ivy towers of the university or just the hollow chatter of another motivational speaker; it is a calling (a Divine imperative) I must fulfill. I've had a seven-fold purpose for presenting these powerful wealth building principles:

✦ To have you receive an anointing and flow of wealth building in your life and to have it flow into the lives of others.

✦ To encourage you to stir up that God-placed, righteous desire within you to produce wealth—and to do it without feeling guilty, unspiritual, or undeserving. I firmly believe human beings are *obligated* to produce wealth. Our EKG'S (Experiences, Knowledge, Gifts, and Skills) and God-given abilities mandate this.

✦ To present powerful, enlightening, and accurate wealth interpretations and applications of the Scriptures, which many believers have misinterpreted or overlooked.

✦ To eradicate poverty thinking (stinkin' thinkin') from your life.

✦ To encourage you to express your UPT (Unique Personal Touch) to the world and move forward in your business venture, career change, or personal life with faith and boldness.

✦ To have you understand and practice the dynamic principles of the P.I.E.S.—God's Wealth Cycle (Producing, Increasing, Enjoying, and Sharing wealth) because it holds the keys to your wealth future.

✦ To show you how to make a full commitment to modeling wealthy attitudes and habits that support personal, social, and economic prosperity.

A quote from Dr. Martin Luther King Jr.'s famous, "I Have a Dream" speech delivered on the steps of the Lincoln Memorial in Washington, D.C., on August 28, 1963, will fit nicely here. He stated,

"We cannot be satisfied as long as the Negro's basic mobility is from a smaller ghetto to a larger one. We can never be satisfied as long as a Negro in Mississippi cannot vote and a Negro in New York believes he has nothing for which to vote. No, no, we are not satisfied, and we will not be satisfied until *justice rolls down like waters and righteousness like a mighty stream.*"

The italicized poetic expression above is a quote from that great prophet of justice, Amos (5:24). But, I'll quote it in an economic justice context (prosperity, wealth). And I'll not be satisfied until this message holds true for all. And I hope you will not be satisfied until this prophetic challenge holds true for you, too, personally. By the way, the wealth commentary interpretation of this verse is not a forced one. Certainly, any prophet of justice would also be talking about the welfare and prosperity that are the results of true righteousness flowing within systems and individuals.

The Hebrew words used in this verse also support a wealth interpretation. The Hebrew word *tsedaqah*, generally translated, *righteousness*, is also used to denote *prosperity*, including deliverance or victory. (Lord knows, we certainly do need victory in the financial area of our lives.) Also in this verse is the biblical Hebrew word for justice, *mishpat*, which refers to carrying out civil, religious, political, social, and economic laws uprightly. Thus, *mishpat*, refers to *one's legal and financial rights*.

So, instead of the economic interpretation being a foreign one, it has now shown itself as a vital part of the fabric of this verse and the catalyst for the type of environment the prophet envisions. The prophet Amos had a vision of justice (civil and economic rights) and righteousness (God's deliverance) flowing just as I also have a vision of God's prosperity flowing. It is a beautiful and bountiful sight. This is not merely some futuristic fantasy or whimsy. It is, rather, an obligation and a divine mandate to bring into the reality of human experience. So, you and I must not only be the carriers of the good news of wealth, but the very incarnation of it.

So, I will close with Amos 5:24 in the KHWT (KH Wealth Translation).

But let the economic justice of God's Wealth Cycle
roll down like waters,
and the divine laws of wealth and prosperity
like an ever-flowing stream.
Amos 5:24 (KHWT)

May Success and Prosperity be Yours,

Kenneth Hammonds

Acknowledgments

" I Wish to Thank . . . "

  A KH Quotable Quote

Only a fool says, "I am a self-made person."

Know that the LORD, He is God; It is He who has made us, and not we ourselves.

Psalm 100:3(NKJV)

A book does not come from the mind of its author only. It is the result of interactions and rich relationships with many people. I acknowledge all my family and friends, my teachers, my colleagues in ministry, in education, and in personal coaching. I also acknowledge all the authors of the books who have shaped my life and thought—from Moses and the Hebrew prophets to the writers of the Greek NT to Aristotle and the modern-day masters of motivation and success.

However, I give special acknowledgement to those who have had a more direct influence in the production of this book. I am in the success business, and I know no one is a success alone.

To the memory of Dr. George Lawlor, my college Greek teacher at Cedarville College: I'd like to acknowledge the strong impact of his NT Greek classes. His dignity of life and profound teaching are still alive in my life today. Dr. James Grier, my college teacher of philosophy, always challenged me to think philosophically and holistically about truth and to examine every truth claim by the One who is the Truth. I'd like to thank Bishop Charles E. Blake, pastor of West Angeles Church of God in Christ, for being a spiritual and career mentor for twenty years.

I especially wish to thank the insightful students of God's Principles of Abundance (GPA), my twelve-year Bible study class and the School of Success (SOS), my ten-year success workshop series. *God Wants You to be Wealthy* is a direct result of class discussions, challenges, ideas, profound thoughts, opinions, and the changed lives of the individuals in these classes. I am honored to see these success and wealth principles at work in their lives.

I wish to thank Dr. Bennie Goodwin—a great scholar, educator, and mentor—for editing the early stage of the book manuscript. His encouragement that the title is "relevant to the needs of many people, especially to African Americans and other minorities" was very helpful in confirming God's Will regarding this title. Many thanks also to all the editors and numerous general audience reviewers who examined the manuscript grammatically, theologically, logically, literarily, and motivationally.

My parents, Evelyn and Clarence Hammonds, have given me high quality parenting. I thank them for causing me to understand the deep wealth in loving God, family, and people. I am grateful for the love of my life, my wife, Naomi. I thank her for her undying faithfulness to me, even when we didn't seem to be too *wealthy*. I wish to thank Naomi and my daughters, Chara and Dorielle, for reviewing the early manuscript and offering suggestions for improvement and the encouragement to complete it. They all provide fabulous "family wealth" to my life.

Last, but not least, I wish to acknowledge the Triune God, the Source of all True Wealth, and the Creator and Lover of the universe and humanity. I am always reminded of the wise counsel of Proverbs 3:6 to *acknowledge* God, and He will direct and bless our decisions and the course of our lives. This is His work and I give glory and praise to Him. In the words of the Greeks:

ΔΟΧΑ ΤΩ ΘΕΩ
(doxa tō theō)
English translation: **GLORY TO GOD**

About the Author

Dr. Kenneth Hammonds,
Success & Leadership Coach

General Information

Dr. Kenneth Hammonds is a dynamic speaker, writer, workshop specialist, and a success and leadership coach. He is founder and chief visionary of **Spiritual Empowerment, Plus,** a coaching and training company specializing in personal coaching for individuals and group coaching workshops and seminars for organizations. As a certified success coach and a certified professional behavioral analyst, he specializes in personal, leadership, ministry, and emerging entrepreneurs development for new businesses and ministries. Dr Hammonds is also a New Testament Greek trainer.

Dr. Hammonds implements training programs for large and small organizations and delivers provoking and motivating presentations for the workforce of businesses. He also conducts in-depth assessments and training programs for managers and executives.

Dr. Hammonds has served as a senior management executive, corporate trainer, and curriculum developer for organizations for over twenty years. He is responsible for founding four schools, including the School of Success (SOS), and numerous staff development programs at West Angeles Church of God in Christ (a multimillion-dollar, 20,000 member congregation with over 200 staff members), where he also implemented training programs for over 100 volunteer leaders. These 100+ leaders and managers were responsible for a total volunteer cadre of over 3,000 persons.

Dr. Hammonds is a certified Christian coach. As a personal coach, he helps individuals to live balanced lives and to achieve their personal goals more quickly and with less stress. He designs personalized plans for empowering people to start and complete their important goals and dreams. The "Success Coach" inspires people to move to the next level in their professional and personal lives. His inspiring and encouraging coaching style stirs up and incites thought, innovation, and action, as he coaches with insight, honesty, and empathy. He empowers people to reach God's Best.

He is especially gifted in bringing out the best in people at all social, economic, and spiritual levels. His tactful humor and supportive style will provoke you to productivity, profitability, and excellence in the workplace and in life.

He also empowers leaders to clarify and achieve organizational goals and develop personal and organizational mission statements. He develops executives into more effective leaders who are able to coach and motivate staff toward productivity, profitability, and excellence.

Dr. Hammonds' mission and calling is *to bring out the best in individuals and to organize individuals, families, and organizations for success.*

Education
Dr. Hammonds holds a BA, M.Div. (philosophy/theology degree) and a Doctorate (Ed.D.) in Educational Administration. Dr. Hammonds was honored to be included in the 1989–1990 "Who's Who in American Education."

Professional Coach Training
Graduate of Coach University (An outstanding, world-class personal
   coach training system)
Certified Christian Coach (Christian Coaches Network, a premier
   international Christian Coaching organization)
Member of the ICF (International Coaching Federation)
Member of the Black Professional Coaches Alliance (BPCA)
Certified Personality Profile Consultant
Certified Toleration Specialist
Knowledge Base of over ninety Effective Coaching Skills

Dr. Kenneth Hammonds, The Coach

Spiritual Empowerment, Plus

A COACHING & TRAINING COMPANY

"Empowering People to Reach God's Best"

> **"Nothing happens without. . .**
>
> *Personal Transformation."*

So says Dr. W. Edwards Deming, the father and expert of modern quality control management for businesses. He is called by some the *Mozart of Quality Control.* Dr. Deming's philosophy and values of quality management and business practices can be applied to personal transformation and an improved quality of life for everyone.

In order to see rapid, massive, and sustained progress in your life and success in your business or professional life, there must be personal transformation before reaching your goals and a **coach** to get you there.

This is where the dynamic workshop and speaking services of *Dr. Kenneth Hammonds, The Coach,* will assist you and your organization in reaching your goals and being motivated thorough information and inspiration.

Dr. Kenneth Hammonds
~ A Powerfully Endorsed Ministry ~

See what *Bishop Charles E. Blake,* says regarding the ministry of Dr. Hammonds. Bishop is the pastor of the 20,000-member West Angeles Church of God in Christ and Second Vice President of one of the largest Pentecostal denominations in the world, *The Church of God in Christ.*

"For 17 years Dr. Hammonds has served this organization with distinction and dignity; and he has been instrumental in teaching and developing thousands of individuals to grow and fully develop in the area of their God-given calling. His innovative and creative ideas helped to propel our rapid growth here at West Angeles."

This Coaching and Training Company presents the best in dynamic Spirit-filled presentations and empowerment training in five areas: **Success, Leadership, Christian Living, Personal & Group Coaching, and New Testament Greek.**

Empowerment for Successful Living

"God wants your life to be a success, NOT a mess."

This is the famous motivational quote of Dr. Hammonds. This motivation quip summarizes the philosophy and power of personal transformation to bring success and empowerment in your everyday life. Get your life and the people of your organization motivated and headed for success in their lives through these and many other programs and presentations. Dr. Kenneth Hammonds' School of Success (SOS) presents:

- ✦ **12 Core Disciplines of Truly Successful People:** A success system developed by Dr. Hammonds. The themes are organized into four basic areas (called the life quadrant: self disciplines, people disciplines, time disciplines, work/career disciplines). There are three disciplines in each quadrant. The 12 Disciplines (12 CD) help people perform better personally and professionally and enjoy life more consistently.
- ✦ **Seven Life Changing Foundations for Success:** The seven foundations are also a part of the success system. These are the pillars that provide the success mindset necessary for human achievement.

✦ **Living with Mission and Purpose:** Helping Christians understand and live in God's purpose and calling.

✦ **Creating Wealth God's Way:** Based on the groundbreaking motivational book of Dr. Hammonds, *God Wants You to be Wealthy*, this workshop offers to participants a personal workable plan to be more productive financially and in every dimension of life. It helps people in a practical way link spiritual empowerment and economic empowerment. An exciting God Wants You to be Wealthy seminar video is also available.

"Well, you said taking that workshop in Chicago for an hour would change my life—it did."

—*Dr. Michelle Lloyd-Paige, Professor, Calvin College*

Empowerment for Effective Leadership

"True leadership digs deep to discover human potential and then directs and releases it toward a goal."

My statement above reveals the true purpose of leadership. There is nothing more important in the life of any organization than effective leaders and an effective leadership training program. Whether church, business, social club, community group, or government agency—all need effective leaders to carry out their program and policies.

Dr. Hammonds is an expert in leadership training (doctorate in educational administration) and specializes in training church leaders, both volunteer and paid staff. Pastors have called this program "very effective" and "dynamic." This powerful leadership program is available as a weekend program or an ongoing series of several weeks.

✦ **The Perfecting Leadership Success Program for Christian Ministries:** This comprehensive leadership program is designed to assist your church leaders and workers to be more productive in ministry and life. It emphasizes development of personal skills and people skills. It shows your leaders:

- how to develop and enhance their own personal development for effective leadership;
- how to understand and lead people of different personalities; and
- how to be a visionary leader, upholding and enhancing a pastor's vision.

✦ **Seventy-seven Leadership Lessons: Valuable Lessons on Becoming a Successful Christian Leader**

*Church Growth Workshops for
Church Leaders and Church Boards*

✦ **Creative Ideas for Dynamic Church Growth**
✦ **Understanding and Fulfilling the Mission of Your Church**

For more information, call and request a leadership training brochure, or visit Dr. Hammonds' Web site, *KenHammonds.com* (see the *Workshops* section)

Empowerment for Christian Living

*"How can a young man [and any believer] keep his way pure?
By living according to your word."*

Psalm 119:9, NIV

The Christian life is full of challenges for direction and understanding the Will of God. The answer to the Christian's effective walk with God for today's modern challenges is a clearer understanding of the Word of God placed in a modern setting and brought forth dynamically and motivationally with power and anointing.

Dr. Hammonds has been a Christian educator for over thirty years and led the Education Department of one of the largest churches in America for seventeen years. His workshops are known for the combination of in-depth study of Scripture, with inspiration, motivation, and humor. Each presentation is presented with practical, real-life examples and application to everyday life. Dr. Hammonds' workshops cover nearly every area of Christian living.

Here is a sampling of these dynamic workshop topics:

+ **How to Enjoy a Happy Married Life and Lovemaking in the Bible**
+ **Seven Tips on Getting Information from the Bible**
+ **The Sunday School Workshop: Dynamic Sunday School Training for Today's Church**
+ **How to be a Marrying Kinda' Guy** (for single men only)

"We would like to thank you for blessing our Church family along with others who attended the Marriage Seminar. I appreciate you allowing the Lord to use you and your wife. The married couples are still talking about lovemaking in the Bible. The Conference was great!"

—*Pastor Don Jones*

For more information regarding Dr. Hammonds' numerous workshops, request information or visit his Web site *KenHammonds.com* (see the *Workshops* section). Some special workshops can be designed upon request.

Personal & Group Coaching Empowerment for Personal Growth

"Get on the cutting-edge in ministry and in life—get a coach!"

The key to moving your life forward when you are stuck or seeking direction is the encouragement of a professional Christian Coach. Dr. Hammonds specializes in those in life transitions and those beginning solo businesses. Your personal or professional goals can be reached more quickly and easily with the help of a professionally trained coach.

For me, coaching is much more than just a profession—it is a calling and a gift that I have cultivated and honed through years of ministry experience and professional training through Coach University, the premier coach training program in the world, and training in the application of the more than ninety coaching skills.

Listed below are some of the twenty assessments utilized in my personal and group coaching sessions:

+ **Clean Sweep Program:** A personal life balance tool that assesses your life in four areas
+ **Executive and Staff Personality Profile:** Dr. Hammonds is a Certified Personality Profile Consultant.
+ **Staff Excellence Program:** A program for church paid staff managers and executives to improve their skills
+ **New Business Start-Up Program:** A program for beginning entrepreneurs

For more information regarding Dr. Hammonds' coaching ministry, request information or visit his Web site *KenHammonds.com.* (see the *KH's Coaching Ministry* section).

"I was also honored to be a small part of the beginnings of your coaching ministry. It was an amazing time in my life when so many of my goals were coming to fruition, and your coaching was vital to helping me to stay focused, confident, and to containing the anxiety that could have easily unraveled me."
—Dr. Cindy Scott, Psychologist, Hirsch Psychological Services

Empowerment in the Scriptures:
NT Greek Training for Ministry

Apollos in Acts 18:24 is described in the Greek text as:
dynatos en tais graphais: **powerful [empowered] in the Scriptures.**

Do you want to be more empowered in the Scriptures? Well, an introduction to word studies in the NT Greek will take you there. (Actually, the *real* New Testament is the Greek New Testament—all else is merely a translation.)

Dr. Hammonds has over thirty-five years of study and teaching in New Testament Greek and has developed his expertise as the **New Testament Greek Trainer**. His very practical approach to the study of the Greek New Testament is revealed in his outstanding and groundbreaking book, *An Introduction to New Testament Greek Word Studies: A New Approach to Word Studies in the Greek New Testament.*

The Spirit-filled presentations of this practical approach to the study of the Word of God has been described by students as "life changing." Greek Training has moved to a new level with the coming to the science of Dr. Hammonds' famous "Greek in a Week" workshops.

One participant described the experience in one of Dr. Hammonds' workshops in this way:

"You are clever, witty, and skillful in all aspects of executive performance. Your exceptional intelligence, creativity, hard work, perseverance, and judgment make you an outstanding example of ministerial leadership AT ITS BEST! Your spiritual fervor is contagious…and I'm catching It! Thank you for being such a marvelous Christian education teacher."

Experience the joy and the depth of Biblical and practical knowledge for yourself, your church congregation, or your organization though the powerful and dynamic coaching and training ministry of Dr. Kenneth Hammonds. Contact Dr. Hammonds today for a quality, powerful, in-depth, and dynamic presentation.

FOR ORDERING

God Wants You to be Wealthy

By Dr. Kenneth Hammonds

Call **800-247-6553** for quick service and shipping of your order.
Fax orders to **419-281-6883**.

You can also order this dynamic book online at:
WealthyThinking.com

For more information, contact:

Dr. Kenneth Hammonds

Spiritual Empowerment, Plus
P.O. Box 2853 Inglewood, CA 90305-0853
Email: KH@WealthyThinking.com
Coaching Web site: KenHammonds.com
Phone: 323-753-1366

LEARN THE BASICS OF NEW TESTAMENT GREEK ON YOUR OWN!

AN INTRODUCTION TO NEW TESTAMENT GREEK GRAMMAR FOR WORD STUDIES:

A New Approach to Word Studies in the Greek New Testament

Do you want to research Biblical studies of wealth in New Testament Greek like the studies in this wealth commentary? Get a copy of Dr. Hammonds' NT Greek grammar book, *Introduction to New Testament Greek Grammar for Word Studies.*

This self-study Greek grammar book will show you how to do Greek word studies in the original language of the NT. Get it and other books written by Dr. Hammonds at the coaching Web site *KenHammonds.com.*

This is the Only Book to Use This Approach to Word Studies.

✦ No more "Webster says" but, "God says."
✦ Learn Greek with this new approach to studying NT Greek.
✦ Cut your study time of Greek in half or even less.
✦ Locate any word in the Greek NT and identify its form.
✦ Do introductory level exposition and exegesis.
✦ Utilize the better Biblical commentaries and theological works.

Get deep into the Word in the original language.

Used successfully for over twenty years.
Get it today and get into the Word!

Be truly: *dynatos en tais graphais:* **powerful in the Scriptures** (Apollos: Acts 18:24)

MORE ADVANCE ACCLAIM FROM READERS AND EDITORS FOR:

God Wants You to be Wealthy

"After reading the book it has given me new insight and determination to continue seeking and to obtain the wealth that's for me. Wow, this book is one of the greatest books I have read in a very long time. Next to the Word of God, Dr. Hammonds, this book has opened my eyes to the real life. Tremendous Book!!!!!!"

> **Nathersea Pascascio**, Single mother starting a women's ministry

"Enjoyed reading! Once I started to flow, I couldn't stop reading!"

> **Pastor Glen Garcia**, Associate Pastor

"Dr. Ken, you have done it again! Once again, you have motivated me to do more with what God has given me. Your book, *God Wants You to be Wealthy*, helped me to understand that God really, really has given me the power to obtain wealth. I better understand that 'I' have in my house and being the 'things' that can produce wealth. I enjoyed P.I.E.S (and I thought they were only good for food!)."

> **Michelle R. Loyd-Paige, Ph.D.**, Professor of Sociology, Calvin College Founder of Preach Sista Ministries, PreachSista.com

- "I particularly like how the ten principles that the widow applied are broken down so that we can apply these principles to our lives. I particularly enjoyed wealth-building Secret #2—to use what I have—no matter how small it may seem. That section is very encouraging.

- Wow! What an introduction. I particularly liked how you explained that your book is not for everyone. How true. It is only for the person who has a particular mindset.

- Very readable. I thought that the handling of the Scriptures was quite sound. I particularly found the definition of talent quite interesting, and I liked the translation into today's dollars."

> **Valerie Clayton**, Author, Co-author of *Victory in Singleness*

"Praise God. . . .Everyone will need your book, Doc. And if I may say so. . . . every single mother of color (especially us) will need it even more so. . . .THANK YOU, DOC. . . .Wonderful. . . "

> **Pat Howard**, Single Mother, Sales Representative

"*God Wants You to be Wealthy* has the best Scriptures in the subject [of wealth] throughout the book. I rate the book as excellent."

> **Pastor Rodney Atkins**, Pastor, Librarian, and Social Activist

"The content is outstanding! This is the reason I take advantage of every opportunity I can to sit under your teaching."

> **Gwen Davis**, Top-selling Sales Rep, Trainer, and Speaker

She says it was of "tremendous impact" knowing that she was an inheritor of wealth from God, Adam, and Abraham.

> **Ornie Thomas**, Senior Adult Christian

"I found myself writing down notes as I read. It was very thought provoking. The list of references is extremely helpful, and the way it's broken down makes it so easy to go to the needed area to find further materials on the subject. (I thought that was so great!)"

> **Elizabeth Johnson**, Proofreader, Greeting Card Writer

When asked, "What points stand out for you in the chapter?" the response was:

A. "The outcry against minimum wage mentality."

B. "The first metanoia is to know you are self-employed already and your employer . . . is merely one of your clients. REVOLUTIONARY!!!! TALK ABOUT MIND-CHANGING!!!! It's a whole new approach that empowers you and takes you out of the victim/slave mode of thinking."

> **Cecilia Sims**, Editor/Manuscript Writing Designer

"It's a great write and reads very well. Easy to comprehend and yet profound in its ideas. Most importantly, as a book targeted for the Christian enter, many biblical Scriptures give valid foundation of each principle and idea."

Lamont Woodert, College Student, Pepperdine University

"It was a pleasure and a delight reading both the message to readers and Chapter 7 [now Chapter 6]. Your story-telling ability is truly awesome. The book is truly inspiring and easy to read. Many thanks for sharing your teaching with me—I consider myself a student for life."

Willette Wilson-Duvall, Pro-Vision Productions, Gospel Concert Promoter